Spurring
AI Self-Driving
Cars

Practical Advances in
Artificial Intelligence and Machine Learning

Dr. Lance B. Eliot, MBA, PhD

DEDICATION

To my incredible daughter, Lauren, and my incredible son, Michael.

Forest fortuna adiuvat (from the Latin; good fortune favors the brave).

CONTENTS

Lance B. Eliot

ACKNOWLEDGMENTS

I have been the beneficiary of advice and counsel by many friends, colleagues, family, investors, and many others. I want to thank everyone that has aided me throughout my career. I write from the heart and the head, having experienced first-hand what it means to have others around you that support you during the good times and the tough times.

To Warren Bennis, one of my doctoral advisors and ultimately a colleague, I offer my deepest thanks and appreciation, especially for his calm and insightful wisdom and support.

To Mark Stevens and his generous efforts toward funding and supporting the USC Stevens Center for Innovation.

To Lloyd Greif and the USC Lloyd Greif Center for Entrepreneurial Studies for their ongoing encouragement of founders and entrepreneurs.

To Peter Drucker, William Wang, Aaron Levie, Peter Kim, Jon Kraft, Cindy Crawford, Jenny Ming, Steve Milligan, Chis Underwood, Frank Gehry, Buzz Aldrin, Steve Forbes, Bill Thompson, Dave Dillon, Alan Fuerstman, Larry Ellison, Jim Sinegal, John Sperling, Mark Stevenson, Anand Nallathambi, Thomas Barrack, Jr., and many other innovators and leaders that I have met and gained mightily from doing so.

Thanks to Ed Trainor, Kevin Anderson, James Hickey, Wendell Jones, Ken Harris, DuWayne Peterson, Mike Brown, Jim Thornton, Abhi Beniwal, Al Biland, John Nomura, Eliot Weinman, John Desmond, and many others for their unwavering support during my career.

And most of all thanks as always to Michael and Lauren, for their ongoing support and for having seen me writing and heard much of this material during the many months involved in writing it. To their patience and willingness to listen.

Lance B. Eliot

INTRODUCTION

This is a book that provides the newest innovations and the latest Artificial Intelligence (AI) advances about the emerging nature of AI-based autonomous self-driving driverless cars. Via recent advances in Artificial Intelligence (AI) and Machine Learning (ML), we are nearing the day when vehicles can control themselves and will not require and nor rely upon human intervention to perform their driving tasks (or, that <u>allow</u> for human intervention, but only *require* human intervention in very limited ways).

Similar to my other related books, which I describe in a moment and list the chapters in the Appendix A of this book, I am particularly focused on those advances that pertain to self-driving cars. The phrase "autonomous vehicles" is often used to refer to any kind of vehicle, whether it is ground-based or in the air or sea, and whether it is a cargo hauling trailer truck or a conventional passenger car. Though the aspects described in this book are certainly applicable to all kinds of autonomous vehicles, I am focused more so here on cars.

Indeed, I am especially known for my role in aiding the advancement of self-driving cars, serving currently as the Executive Director of the Cybernetic Self-Driving Cars Institute.. In addition to writing software, designing and developing systems and software for self-driving cars, I also speak and write quite a bit about the topic. This book is a collection of some of my more advanced essays. For those of you that might have seen my essays posted elsewhere, I have updated them and integrated them into this book as one handy cohesive package.

You might be interested in companion books that I have written that provide additional key innovations and fundamentals about self-driving cars. Those books are entitled **"Introduction to Driverless Self-Driving Cars," "Advances in AI and Autonomous Vehicles: Cybernetic Self-Driving Cars," "Self-Driving Cars: "The Mother of All AI Projects," "Innovation and Thought Leadership on Self-Driving Driverless Cars," "New Advances in AI Autonomous Driverless Self-Driving Cars,"** and **"Autonomous Vehicle Driverless Self-Driving Cars and**

Artificial Intelligence," "Transformative Artificial Intelligence Driverless Self-Driving Cars," "Disruptive Artificial Intelligence and Driverless Self-Driving Cars, and "State-of-the-Art AI Driverless Self-Driving Cars," and "Top Trends in AI Self-Driving Cars," and "AI Innovations and Self-Driving Cars," "Crucial Advances for AI Driverless Cars," "Sociotechnical Insights and AI Driverless Cars," "Pioneering Advances for AI Driverless Cars" and "Leading Edge Trends for AI Driverless Cars," "The Cutting Edge of AI Autonomous Cars" and "The Next Wave of AI Self-Driving Cars" and "Revolutionary Innovations of AI Self-Driving Cars," and "AI Self-Driving Cars Breakthroughs," "Trailblazing Trends for AI Self-Driving Cars," "Ingenious Strides for AI Driverless Cars," "AI Self-Driving Cars Inventiveness," "Visionary Secrets of AI Driverless Cars," "Spearheading AI Self-Driving Cars," "Spurring AI Self-Driving Cars" (they are all available via Amazon). Appendix A has a listing of the chapters covered in those books.

For the introduction herein to this book, I am going to borrow my introduction from those companion books, since it does a good job of laying out the landscape of self-driving cars and my overall viewpoints on the topic. The remainder of the book is all new material that does not appear in the companion books.

INTRODUCTION TO SELF-DRIVING CARS

This is a book about self-driving cars. Someday in the future, we'll all have self-driving cars and this book will perhaps seem antiquated, but right now, we are at the forefront of the self-driving car wave. Daily news bombards us with flashes of new announcements by one car maker or another and leaves the impression that within the next few weeks or maybe months that the self-driving car will be here. A casual non-technical reader would assume from these news flashes that in fact we must be on the cusp of a true self-driving car.

Here's a real news flash: We are still quite a distance from having a true self-driving car. It is years to go before we get there.

Why is that? Because a true self-driving car is akin to a moonshot. In the same manner that getting us to the moon was an incredible feat, likewise is achieving a true self-driving car. Anybody that suggests or even brashly states that the true self-driving car is nearly here should be viewed with great skepticism. Indeed, you'll see that I often tend to use the word "hogwash" or "crock" when I assess much of the decidedly *fake news* about self-driving cars. Those of us on the inside know that what is often reported to the outside is malarkey. Few of the insiders are willing to say so. I have no such hesitation.

Indeed, I've been writing a popular blog post about self-driving cars and hitting hard on those that try to wave their hands and pretend that we are on the imminent verge of true self-driving cars. For many years, I've been known as the AI Insider. Besides writing about AI, I also develop AI software. I do what I describe. It also gives me insights into what others that are doing AI are really doing versus what it is said they are doing.

Many faithful readers had asked me to pull together my insightful short essays and put them into another book, which you are now holding.

For those of you that have been reading my essays over the years, this collection not only puts them together into one handy package, I also updated the essays and added new material. For those of you that are new to the topic of self-driving cars and AI, I hope you find these essays approachable and informative. I also tend to have a writing style with a bit of a voice, and so you'll see that I am times have a wry sense of humor and poke at conformity.

As a former professor and founder of an AI research lab, I for many years wrote in the formal language of academic writing. I published in referred journals and served as an editor for several AI journals. This writing here is not of the nature, and I have adopted a different and more informal style for these essays. That being said, I also do mention from time-to-time more rigorous material on AI and encourage you all to dig into those deeper and more formal materials if so interested.

I am also an AI practitioner. This means that I write AI software for a living. Currently, I head-up the Cybernetics Self-Driving Car Institute, where we are developing AI software for self-driving cars. I am excited to also report that my son, also a software engineer, heads-up our Cybernetics Self-Driving Car Lab. What I have helped to start, and for which he is an integral part, ultimately he will carry long into the future after I have retired. My daughter, a marketing whiz, also is integral to our efforts as head of our Marketing group. She too will carry forward the legacy now being formulated.

For those of you that are reading this book and have a penchant for writing code, you might consider taking a look at the open source code available for self-driving cars. This is a handy place to start learning how to develop AI for self-driving cars. There are also many new educational courses spring forth. There is a growing body of those wanting to learn about and develop self-driving cars, and a growing body of colleges, labs, and other avenues by which you can learn about self-driving cars.

This book will provide a foundation of aspects that I think will get you ready for those kinds of more advanced training opportunities. If you've already taken those classes, you'll likely find these essays especially interesting as they offer a perspective that I am betting few other instructors or faculty offered to you. These are challenging essays that ask you to think beyond the conventional about self-driving cars.

THE MOTHER OF ALL AI PROJECTS

In June 2017, Apple CEO Tim Cook came out and finally admitted that Apple has been working on a self-driving car. As you'll see in my essays, Apple was enmeshed in secrecy about their self-driving car efforts. We have only been able to read the tea leaves and guess at what Apple has been up to. The notion of an iCar has been floating for quite a while, and self-driving engineers and researchers have been signing tight-lipped Non-Disclosure Agreements (NDA's) to work on projects at Apple that were as shrouded in mystery as any military invasion plans might be.

Tim Cook said something that many others in the Artificial Intelligence (AI) field have been saying, namely, the creation of a self-driving car has got to be the mother of all AI projects. In other words, it is in fact a tremendous moonshot for AI. If a self-driving car can be crafted and the AI works as we hope, it means that we have made incredible strides with AI and that therefore it opens many other worlds of potential breakthrough accomplishments that AI can solve.

Is this hyperbole? Am I just trying to make AI seem like a miracle worker and so provide self-aggrandizing statements for those of us writing the AI software for self-driving cars? No, it is not hyperbole. Developing a true self-driving car is really, really, really hard to do. Let me take a moment to explain why. As a side note, I realize that the Apple CEO is known for at times uttering hyperbole, and he had previously said for example that the year 2012 was "the mother of all years," and he had said that the release of iOS 10 was "the mother of all releases" – all of which does suggest he likes to use the handy "mother of" expression. But, I assure you, in terms of true self-driving cars, he has hit the nail on the head. For sure.

When you think about a moonshot and how we got to the moon, there are some identifiable characteristics and those same aspects can be applied to creating a true self-driving car. You'll notice that I keep putting the word "true" in front of the self-driving car expression. I do so because as per my essay about the various levels of self-driving cars, there are some self-driving cars that are only somewhat of a self-driving car. The somewhat versions are ones that require a human driver to be ready to intervene. In my view, that's not a true self-driving car. A true self-driving car is one that requires no human driver intervention at all. It is a car that can entirely undertake via automation the driving task without any human driver needed. This is the essence of what is known as a Level 5 self-driving car. We are currently at the Level 2 and Level 3 mark, and not yet at Level 5.

Getting to the moon involved aspects such as having big stretch goals, incremental progress, experimentation, innovation, and so on. Let's review how this applied to the moonshot of the bygone era, and how it applies to the self-driving car moonshot of today.

Big Stretch Goal

Trying to take a human and deliver the human to the moon, and bring them back, safely, was an extremely large stretch goal at the time. No one knew whether it could be done. The technology wasn't available yet. The cost was huge. The determination would need to be fierce. Etc. To reach a Level 5 self-driving car is going to be the same. It is a big stretch goal. We can readily get to the Level 3, and we are able to see the Level 4 just up ahead, but a Level 5 is still an unknown as to if it is doable. It should eventually be doable and in the same way that we thought we'd eventually get to the moon, but when it will occur is a different story.

Incremental Progress

Getting to the moon did not happen overnight in one fell swoop. It took years and years of incremental progress to get there. Likewise for self-driving cars. Google has famously been striving to get to the Level 5, and pretty much been willing to forgo dealing with the intervening levels, but most of the other self-driving car makers are doing the incremental route. Let's get a good Level 2 and a somewhat Level 3 going. Then, let's improve the Level 3 and get a somewhat Level 4 going. Then, let's improve the Level 4 and finally arrive at a Level 5. This seems to be the prevalent way that we are going to achieve the true self-driving car.

Experimentation

You likely know that there were various experiments involved in perfecting the approach and technology to get to the moon. As per making incremental progress, we first tried to see if we could get a rocket to go into space and safety return, then put a monkey in there, then with a human, then we went all the way to the moon but didn't land, and finally we arrived at the mission that actually landed on the moon. Self-driving cars are the same way. We are doing simulations of self-driving cars. We do testing of self-driving cars on private land under controlled situations. We do testing of self-driving cars on public roadways, often having to meet regulatory requirements including for example having an engineer or equivalent in the car to take over the controls if needed. And so on. Experiments big and small are needed to figure out what works and what doesn't.

Innovation

There are already some advances in AI that are allowing us to progress toward self-driving cars. We are going to need even more advances. Innovation in all aspects of technology are going to be required to achieve a true self-driving car. By no means do we already have everything in-hand that we need to get there. Expect new inventions and new approaches, new algorithms, etc.

Setbacks

Most of the pundits are avoiding talking about potential setbacks in the progress toward self-driving cars. Getting to the moon involved many setbacks, some of which you never have heard of and were buried at the time so as to not dampen enthusiasm and funding for getting to the moon. A recurring theme in many of my included essays is that there are going to be setbacks as we try to arrive at a true self-driving car. Take a deep breath and be ready. I just hope the setbacks don't completely stop progress. I am sure that it will cause progress to alter in a manner that we've not yet seen in the self-driving car field. I liken the self-driving car of today to the excitement everyone had for Uber when it first got going. Today, we have a different view of Uber and with each passing day there are more regulations to the ride sharing business and more concerns raised. The darling child only stays a darling until finally that child acts up. It will happen the same with self-driving cars.

SELF-DRIVING CARS CHALLENGES

But what exactly makes things so hard to have a true self-driving car, you might be asking. You have seen cruise control for years and years. You've lately seen cars that can do parallel parking. You've seen YouTube videos of Tesla drivers that put their hands out the window as their car zooms along the highway, and seen to therefore be in a self-driving car. Aren't we just needing to put a few more sensors onto a car and then we'll have in-hand a true self-driving car? Nope.

Consider for a moment the nature of the driving task. We don't just let anyone at any age drive a car. Worldwide, most countries won't license a driver until the age of 18, though many do allow a learner's permit at the age of 15 or 16. Some suggest that a younger age would be physically too small to reach the controls of the car. Though this might be the case, we could easily adjust the controls to allow for younger aged and thus smaller stature. It's not their physical size that matters. It's their cognitive development that matters.

To drive a car, you need to be able to reason about the car, what the car can and cannot do. You need to know how to operate the car. You need to know about how other cars on the road drive. You need to know what is allowed in driving such as speed limits and driving within marked lanes. You need to be able to react to situations and be able to avoid getting into accidents. You need to ascertain when to hit your brakes, when to steer clear of a pedestrian, and how to keep from ramming that motorcyclist that just cut you off.

Many of us had taken courses on driving. We studied about driving and took driver training. We had to take a test and pass it to be able to drive. The point being that though most adults take the driving task for granted, and we often "mindlessly" drive our cars, there is a significant amount of cognitive effort that goes into driving a car. After a while, it becomes second nature. You don't especially think about how you drive, you just do it. But, if you watch a novice driver, say a teenager learning to drive, you suddenly realize that there is a lot more complexity to it than we seem to realize.

Furthermore, driving is a very serious task. I recall when my daughter and son first learned to drive. They are both very conscientious people. They wanted to make sure that whatever they did, they did well, and that they did not harm anyone. Every day, when you get into a car, it is probably around 4,000 pounds of hefty metal and plastics (about two tons), and it is a lethal weapon. Think about it. You drive down the street in an object that weighs two tons and with the engine it can accelerate and ram into anything you want to hit. The damage a car can inflict is very scary. Both my children were surprised that they were being given the right to maneuver this monster of a beast that could cause tremendous harm entirely by merely letting go of the steering wheel for a moment or taking your eyes off the road.

In fact, in the United States alone there are about 30,000 deaths per year by auto accidents, which is around 100 per day. Given that there are about 263 million cars in the United States, I am actually more amazed that the number of fatalities is not a lot higher. During my morning commute, I look at all the thousands of cars on the freeway around me, and I think that if all of them decided to go zombie and drive in a crazy maniac way, there would be many people dead. Somehow, incredibly, each day, most people drive relatively safely. To me, that's a miracle right there. Getting millions and millions of people to be safe and sane when behind the wheel of a two ton mobile object, it's a feat that we as a society should admire with pride.

So, hopefully you are in agreement that the driving task requires a great deal of cognition. You don't' need to be especially smart to drive a car, and we've done quite a bit to make car driving viable for even the average dolt. There isn't an IQ test that you need to take to drive a car. If you can read and write, and pass a test, you pretty much can legally drive a car. There are of course some that drive a car and are not legally permitted to do so, plus there are private areas such as farms where drivers are young, but for public roadways in the United States, you can be generally of average intelligence (or less) and be able to legally drive.

This though makes it seem like the cognitive effort must not be much. If the cognitive effort was truly hard, wouldn't we only have Einstein's that could drive a car? We have made sure to keep the driving task as simple as we can, by making the controls easy and relatively standardized, and by having roads that are relatively standardized, and so on. It is as though Disneyland has put their Autopia into the real-world, by us all as a society agreeing that roads will be a certain way, and we'll all abide by the various rules of driving.

A modest cognitive task by a human is still something that stymies AI. You certainly know that AI has been able to beat chess players and be good at other kinds of games. This type of narrow cognition is not what car driving is about. Car driving is much wider. It requires knowledge about the world, which a chess playing AI system does not need to know. The cognitive aspects of driving are on the one hand seemingly simple, but at the same time require layer upon layer of knowledge about cars, people, roads, rules, and a myriad of other "common sense" aspects. We don't have any AI systems today that have that same kind of breadth and depth of awareness and knowledge.

As revealed in my essays, the self-driving car of today is using trickery to do particular tasks. It is all very narrow in operation. Plus, it currently assumes that a human driver is ready to intervene. It is like a child that we have taught to stack blocks, but we are needed to be right there in case the child stacks them too high and they begin to fall over. AI of today is brittle, it is narrow, and it does not approach the cognitive abilities of humans. This is why the true self-driving car is somewhere out in the future.

Another aspect to the driving task is that it is not solely a mind exercise. You do need to use your senses to drive. You use your eyes a vision sensors to see the road ahead. You vision capability is like a streaming video, which your brain needs to continually analyze as you drive. Where is the road? Is there a pedestrian in the way? Is there another car ahead of you? Your senses are relying a flood of info to your brain. Self-driving cars are trying to do the same, by using cameras, radar, ultrasound, and lasers. This is an attempt at mimicking how humans have senses and sensory apparatus.

Thus, the driving task is mental and physical. You use your senses, you use your arms and legs to manipulate the controls of the car, and you use your brain to assess the sensory info and direct your limbs to act upon the controls of the car. This all happens instantly. If you've ever perhaps gotten something in your eye and only had one eye available to drive with, you suddenly realize how dependent upon vision you are. If you have a broken foot with a cast, you suddenly realize how hard it is to control the brake pedal and the accelerator. If you've taken medication and your brain is maybe sluggish, you suddenly realize how much mental strain is required to drive a car.

An AI system that plays chess only needs to be focused on playing chess. The physical aspects aren't important because usually a human moves the chess pieces or the chessboard is shown on an electronic display. Using AI for a more life-and-death task such as analyzing MRI images of patients, this again does not require physical capabilities and instead is done by examining images of bits.

Driving a car is a true life-and-death task. It is a use of AI that can easily and at any moment produce death. For those colleagues of mine that are developing this AI, as am I, we need to keep in mind the somber aspects of this. We are producing software that will have in its virtual hands the lives of the occupants of the car, and the lives of those in other nearby cars, and the lives of nearby pedestrians, etc. Chess is not usually a life-or-death matter.

Driving is all around us. Cars are everywhere. Most of today's AI applications involve only a small number of people. Or, they are behind the scenes and we as humans have other recourse if the AI messes up. AI that is driving a car at 80 miles per hour on a highway had better not mess up. The consequences are grave. Multiply this by the number of cars, if we could put magically self-driving into every car in the USA, we'd have AI running in the 263 million cars. That's a lot of AI spread around. This is AI on a massive scale that we are not doing today and that offers both promise and potential peril.

There are some that want AI for self-driving cars because they envision a world without any car accidents. They envision a world in which there is no car congestion and all cars cooperate with each other. These are wonderful utopian visions.

They are also very misleading. The adoption of self-driving cars is going to be incremental and not overnight. We cannot economically just junk all existing cars. Nor are we going to be able to affordably retrofit existing cars. It is more likely that self-driving cars will be built into new cars and that over many years of gradual replacement of existing cars that we'll see the mix of self-driving cars become substantial in the real-world.

In these essays, I have tried to offer technological insights without being overly technical in my description, and also blended the business, societal, and economic aspects too. Technologists need to consider the non-technological impacts of what they do. Non-technologists should be aware of what is being developed.

We all need to work together to collectively be prepared for the enormous disruption and transformative aspects of true self-driving cars. We all need to be involved in this mother of all AI projects.

WHAT THIS BOOK PROVIDES

What does this book provide to you? It introduces many of the key elements about self-driving cars and does so with an AI based perspective. I weave together technical and non-technical aspects, readily going from being concerned about the cognitive capabilities of the driving task and how the technology is embodying this into self-driving cars, and in the next breath I discuss the societal and economic aspects.

They are all intertwined because that's the way reality is. You cannot separate out the technology per se, and instead must consider it within the milieu of what is being invented and innovated, and do so with a mindset towards the contemporary mores and culture that shape what we are doing and what we hope to do.

WHY THIS BOOK

I wrote this book to try and bring to the public view many aspects about self-driving cars that nobody seems to be discussing.

For business leaders that are either involved in making self-driving cars or that are going to leverage self-driving cars, I hope that this book will enlighten you as to the risks involved and ways in which you should be strategizing about how to deal with those risks.

For entrepreneurs, startups and other businesses that want to enter into the self-driving car market that is emerging, I hope this book sparks your interest in doing so, and provides some sense of what might be prudent to pursue.

For researchers that study self-driving cars, I hope this book spurs your interest in the risks and safety issues of self-driving cars, and also nudges you toward conducting research on those aspects.

For students in computer science or related disciplines, I hope this book will provide you with interesting and new ideas and material, for which you might conduct research or provide some career direction insights for you.

For AI companies and high-tech companies pursuing self-driving cars, this book will hopefully broaden your view beyond just the mere coding and development needed to make self-driving cars.

For all readers, I hope that you will find the material in this book to be stimulating. Some of it will be repetitive of things you already know. But I am pretty sure that you'll also find various eureka moments whereby you'll discover a new technique or approach that you had not earlier thought of. I am also betting that there will be material that forces you to rethink some of your current practices.

I am not saying you will suddenly have an epiphany and change what you are doing. I do think though that you will reconsider or perhaps revisit what you are doing.

For anyone choosing to use this book for teaching purposes, please take a look at my suggestions for doing so, as described in the Appendix. I have found the material handy in courses that I have taught, and likewise other faculty have told me that they have found the material handy, in some cases as extended readings and in other instances as a core part of their course (depending on the nature of the class).

In my writing for this book, I have tried carefully to blend both the practitioner and the academic styles of writing. It is not as dense as is typical academic journal writing, but at the same time offers depth by going into the nuances and trade-offs of various practices.

The word "deep" is in vogue today, meaning getting deeply into a subject or topic, and so is the word "unpack" which means to tease out the underlying aspects of a subject or topic. I have sought to offer material that addresses an issue or topic by going relatively deeply into it and make sure that it is well unpacked.

Finally, in any book about AI, it is difficult to use our everyday words without having some of them be misinterpreted. Specifically, it is easy to anthropomorphize AI. When I say that an AI system "knows" something, I do not want you to construe that the AI system has sentience and "knows" in the same way that humans do. They aren't that way, as yet. I have tried to use quotes around such words from time-to-time to emphasize that the words I am using should not be misinterpreted to ascribe true human intelligence to the AI systems that we know of today. If I used quotes around all such words, the book would be very difficult to read, and so I am doing so judiciously. Please keep that in mind as you read the material, thanks.

COMPANION BOOKS

If you find this material of interest, you might enjoy these too:

1. "Introduction to Driverless Self-Driving Cars" by Dr. Lance Eliot
2. "Innovation and Thought Leadership on Self-Driving Driverless Cars" by Dr. Lance Eliot
3. "Advances in AI and Autonomous Vehicles: Cybernetic Self-Driving Cars" by Dr. Lance Eliot
4. "Self-Driving Cars: The Mother of All AI Projects" by Dr. Lance Eliot
5. "New Advances in AI Autonomous Driverless Self-Driving Cars" by Dr. Lance Eliot
6. "Autonomous Vehicle Driverless Self-Driving Cars and Artificial Intelligence" by Dr. Lance Eliot and Michael B. Eliot
7. "Transformative Artificial Intelligence Driverless Self-Driving Cars" by Dr. Lance Eliot
8. "Disruptive Artificial Intelligence and Driverless Self-Driving Cars" by Dr. Lance Eliot
9. "State-of-the-Art AI Driverless Self-Driving Cars" by Dr. Lance Eliot
10. "Top Trends in AI Self-Driving Cars" by Dr. Lance Eliot
11. "AI Innovations and Self-Driving Cars" by Dr. Lance Eliot
12. "Crucial Advances for AI Driverless Cars" by Dr. Lance Eliot
13. "Sociotechnical Insights and AI Driverless Cars" by Dr. Lance Eliot.
14. "Pioneering Advances for AI Driverless Cars" by Dr. Lance Eliot
15. "Leading Edge Trends for AI Driverless Cars" by Dr. Lance Eliot
16. "The Cutting Edge of AI Autonomous Cars" by Dr. Lance Eliot
17. "The Next Wave of AI Self-Driving Cars" by Dr. Lance Eliot
18. "Revolutionary Innovations of AI Driverless Cars" by Dr. Lance Eliot
19. "AI Self-Driving Cars Breakthroughs" by Dr. Lance Eliot
20. "Trailblazing Trends for AI Self-Driving Cars" by Dr. Lance Eliot
21. "Ingenious Strides for AI Driverless Cars" by Dr. Lance Eliot
22. "AI Self-Driving Cars Inventiveness" by Dr. Lance Eliot
23. "Visionary Secrets of AI Driverless Cars" by Dr. Lance Eliot
24. "Spearheading AI Self-Driving Cars" by Dr. Lance Eliot
25. "Spurring AI Self-Driving Cars" by Dr. Lance Eliot

These books are available on Amazon and at other major global booksellers.

CHAPTER 1

ELIOT FRAMEWORK FOR AI SELF-DRIVING CARS

CHAPTER 1

ELIOT FRAMEWORK FOR AI SELF-DRIVING CARS

This chapter is a core foundational aspect for understanding AI self-driving cars and I have used this same chapter in several of my other books to introduce the reader to essential elements of this field. Once you've read this chapter, you'll be prepared to read the rest of the material since the foundational essence of the components of autonomous AI driverless self-driving cars will have been established for you.

———————

When I give presentations about self-driving cars and teach classes on the topic, I have found it helpful to provide a framework around which the various key elements of self-driving cars can be understood and organized (see diagram at the end of this chapter). The framework needs to be simple enough to convey the overarching elements, but at the same time not so simple that it belies the true complexity of self-driving cars. As such, I am going to describe the framework here and try to offer in a thousand words (or more!) what the framework diagram itself intends to portray.

The core elements on the diagram are numbered for ease of reference. The numbering does not suggest any kind of prioritization of the elements. Each element is crucial. Each element has a purpose, and otherwise would not be included in the framework. For some self-driving cars, a particular element might be more important or somehow distinguished in comparison to other self-driving cars.

You could even use the framework to rate a particular self-driving car, doing so by gauging how well it performs in each of the elements of the framework. I will describe each of the elements, one at a time. After doing so, I'll discuss aspects that illustrate how the elements interact and perform during the overall effort of a self-driving car.

At the Cybernetic Self-Driving Car Institute, we use the framework to keep track of what we are working on, and how we are developing software that fills in what is needed to achieve Level 5 self-driving cars.

D-01: Sensor Capture

Let's start with the one element that often gets the most attention in the press about self-driving cars, namely, the sensory devices for a self-driving car.

On the framework, the box labeled as D-01 indicates "Sensor Capture" and refers to the processes of the self-driving car that involve collecting data from the myriad of sensors that are used for a self-driving car. The types of devices typically involved are listed, such as the use of mono cameras, stereo cameras, LIDAR devices, radar systems, ultrasonic devices, GPS, IMU, and so on.

These devices are tasked with obtaining data about the status of the self-driving car and the world around it. Some of the devices are continually providing updates, while others of the devices await an indication by the self-driving car that the device is supposed to collect data. The data might be first transformed in some fashion by the device itself, or it might instead be fed directly into the sensor capture as raw data. At that point, it might be up to the sensor capture processes to do transformations on the data. This all varies depending upon the nature of the devices being used and how the devices were designed and developed.

D-02: Sensor Fusion

Imagine that your eyeballs receive visual images, your nose receives odors, your ears receive sounds, and in essence each of your distinct sensory devices is getting some form of input. The input befits the nature of the device. Likewise, for a self-driving car, the cameras provide visual images, the radar returns radar reflections, and so on.

Each device provides the data as befits what the device does.

At some point, using the analogy to humans, you need to merge together what your eyes see, what your nose smells, what your ears hear, and piece it all together into a larger sense of what the world is all about and what is happening around you. Sensor fusion is the action of taking the singular aspects from each of the devices and putting them together into a larger puzzle.

Sensor fusion is a tough task. There are some devices that might not be working at the time of the sensor capture. Or, there might some devices that are unable to report well what they have detected. Again, using a human analogy, suppose you are in a dark room and so your eyes cannot see much. At that point, you might need to rely more so on your ears and what you hear. The same is true for a self-driving car. If the cameras are obscured due to snow and sleet, it might be that the radar can provide a greater indication of what the external conditions consist of.

In the case of a self-driving car, there can be a plethora of such sensory devices. Each is reporting what it can. Each might have its difficulties. Each might have its limitations, such as how far ahead it can detect an object. All of these limitations need to be considered during the sensor fusion task.

D-03: Virtual World Model

For humans, we presumably keep in our minds a model of the world around us when we are driving a car. In your mind, you know that the car is going at say 60 miles per hour and that you are on a freeway. You have a model in your mind that your car is surrounded by other cars, and that there are lanes to the freeway. Your model is not only based on what you can see, hear, etc., but also what you know about the nature of the world. You know that at any moment that car ahead of you can smash on its brakes, or the car behind you can ram into your car, or that the truck in the next lane might swerve into your lane.

The AI of the self-driving car needs to have a virtual world model, which it then keeps updated with whatever it is receiving from the sensor fusion, which received its input from the sensor capture and the sensory devices.

D-04: System Action Plan

By having a virtual world model, the AI of the self-driving car is able to keep track of where the car is and what is happening around the car. In addition, the AI needs to determine what to do next. Should the self-driving car hit its brakes? Should the self-driving car stay in its lane or swerve into the lane to the left? Should the self-driving car accelerate or slow down?

A system action plan needs to be prepared by the AI of the self-driving car. The action plan specifies what actions should be taken. The actions need to pertain to the status of the virtual world model. Plus, the actions need to be realizable.

This realizability means that the AI cannot just assert that the self-driving car should suddenly sprout wings and fly. Instead, the AI must be bound by whatever the self-driving car can actually do, such as coming to a halt in a distance of X feet at a speed of Y miles per hour, rather than perhaps asserting that the self-driving car come to a halt in 0 feet as though it could instantaneously come to a stop while it is in motion.

D-05: Controls Activation

The system action plan is implemented by activating the controls of the car to act according to what the plan stipulates. This might mean that the accelerator control is commanded to increase the speed of the car. Or, the steering control is commanded to turn the steering wheel 30 degrees to the left or right.

One question arises as to whether or not the controls respond as they are commanded to do. In other words, suppose the AI has commanded the accelerator to increase, but for some reason it does not do so. Or, maybe it tries to do so, but the speed of the car does not increase. The controls activation feeds back into the virtual world model, and simultaneously the virtual world model is getting updated from the sensors, the sensor capture, and the sensor fusion. This allows the AI to ascertain what has taken place as a result of the controls being commanded to take some kind of action.

By the way, please keep in mind that though the diagram seems to have a linear progression to it, the reality is that these are all aspects of the self-driving car that are happening in parallel and simultaneously. The sensors are capturing data, meanwhile the sensor fusion is taking place, meanwhile the virtual model is being updated, meanwhile the system action plan is being formulated and reformulated, meanwhile the controls are being activated.

This is the same as a human being that is driving a car. They are eyeballing the road, meanwhile they are fusing in their mind the sights, sounds, etc., meanwhile their mind is updating their model of the world around them, meanwhile they are formulating an action plan of what to do, and meanwhile they are pushing their foot onto the pedals and steering the car. In the normal course of driving a car, you are doing all of these at once. I mention this so that when you look at the diagram, you will think of the boxes as processes that are all happening at the same time, and not as though only one happens and then the next.

They are shown diagrammatically in a simplistic manner to help comprehend what is taking place. You though should also realize that they are working in parallel and simultaneous with each other. This is a tough aspect in that the inter-element communications involve latency and other aspects that must be taken into account. There can be delays in one element updating and then sharing its latest status with other elements.

D-06: Automobile & CAN

Contemporary cars use various automotive electronics and a Controller Area Network (CAN) to serve as the components that underlie the driving aspects of a car. There are Electronic Control Units (ECU's) which control subsystems of the car, such as the engine, the brakes, the doors, the windows, and so on.

The elements D-01, D-02, D-03, D-04, D-05 are layered on top of the D-06, and must be aware of the nature of what the D-06 is able to do and not do.

D-07: In-Car Commands

Humans are going to be occupants in self-driving cars. In a Level 5 self-driving car, there must be some form of communication that takes place between the humans and the self-driving car. For example, I go into a self-driving car and tell it that I want to be driven over to Disneyland, and along the way I want to stop at In-and-Out Burger. The self-driving car now parses what I've said and tries to then establish a means to carry out my wishes.

In-car commands can happen at any time during a driving journey. Though my example was about an in-car command when I first got into my self-driving car, it could be that while the self-driving car is carrying out the journey that I change my mind. Perhaps after getting stuck in traffic, I tell the self-driving car to forget about getting the burgers and just head straight over to the theme park. The self-driving car needs to be alert to in-car commands throughout the journey.

D-08: V2X Communications

We will ultimately have self-driving cars communicating with each other, doing so via V2V (Vehicle-to-Vehicle) communications. We will also have self-driving cars that communicate with the roadways and other aspects of the transportation infrastructure, doing so via V2I (Vehicle-to-Infrastructure).

The variety of ways in which a self-driving car will be communicating with other cars and infrastructure is being called V2X, whereby the letter X means whatever else we identify as something that a car should or would want to communicate with. The V2X communications will be taking place simultaneous with everything else on the diagram, and those other elements will need to incorporate whatever it gleans from those V2X communications.

D-09: Deep Learning

The use of Deep Learning permeates all other aspects of the self-driving car. The AI of the self-driving car will be using deep learning to do a better job at the systems action plan, and at the controls activation, and at the sensor fusion, and so on.

Currently, the use of artificial neural networks is the most prevalent form of deep learning. Based on large swaths of data, the neural networks attempt to "learn" from the data and therefore direct the efforts of the self-driving car accordingly.

D-10: Tactical AI

Tactical AI is the element of dealing with the moment-to-moment driving of the self-driving car. Is the self-driving car staying in its lane of the freeway? Is the car responding appropriately to the controls commands? Are the sensory devices working?

For human drivers, the tactical equivalent can be seen when you watch a novice driver such as a teenager that is first driving. They are focused on the mechanics of the driving task, keeping their eye on the road while also trying to properly control the car.

D-11: Strategic AI

The Strategic AI aspects of a self-driving car are dealing with the larger picture of what the self-driving car is trying to do. If I had asked that the self-driving car take me to Disneyland, there is an overall journey map that needs to be kept and maintained.

There is an interaction between the Strategic AI and the Tactical AI. The Strategic AI is wanting to keep on the mission of the driving, while the Tactical AI is focused on the particulars underway in the driving effort. If the Tactical AI seems to wander away from the overarching mission, the Strategic AI wants to see why and get things back on track. If the Tactical AI realizes that there is something amiss on the self-driving car, it needs to alert the Strategic AI accordingly and have an adjustment to the overarching mission that is underway.

D-12: Self-Aware AI

Very few of the self-driving cars being developed are including a Self-Aware AI element, which we at the Cybernetic Self-Driving Car Institute believe is crucial to Level 5 self-driving cars.

The Self-Aware AI element is intended to watch over itself, in the sense that the AI is making sure that the AI is working as intended. Suppose you had a human driving a car, and they were starting to drive erratically. Hopefully, their own self-awareness would make them realize they themselves are driving poorly, such as perhaps starting to fall asleep after having been driving for hours on end. If you had a passenger in the car, they might be able to alert the driver if the driver is starting to do something amiss. This is exactly what the Self-Aware

AI element tries to do, it becomes the overseer of the AI, and tries to detect when the AI has become faulty or confused, and then find ways to overcome the issue.

D-13: Economic

The economic aspects of a self-driving car are not per se a technology aspect of a self-driving car, but the economics do indeed impact the nature of a self-driving car. For example, the cost of outfitting a self-driving car with every kind of possible sensory device is prohibitive, and so choices need to be made about which devices are used. And, for those sensory devices chosen, whether they would have a full set of features or a more limited set of features.

We are going to have self-driving cars that are at the low-end of a consumer cost point, and others at the high-end of a consumer cost point. You cannot expect that the self-driving car at the low-end is going to be as robust as the one at the high-end. I realize that many of the self-driving car pundits are acting as though all self-driving cars will be the same, but they won't be. Just like anything else, we are going to have self-driving cars that have a range of capabilities. Some will be better than others. Some will be safer than others. This is the way of the real-world, and so we need to be thinking about the economics aspects when considering the nature of self-driving cars.

D-14: Societal

This component encompasses the societal aspects of AI which also impacts the technology of self-driving cars. For example, the famous Trolley Problem involves what choices should a self-driving car make when faced with life-and-death matters. If the self-driving car is about to either hit a child standing in the roadway, or instead ram into a tree at the side of the road and possibly kill the humans in the self-driving car, which choice should be made?

We need to keep in mind the societal aspects will underlie the AI of the self-driving car. Whether we are aware of it explicitly or not, the AI will have embedded into it various societal assumptions.

D-15: Innovation

I included the notion of innovation into the framework because we can anticipate that whatever a self-driving car consists of, it will continue to be innovated over time. The self-driving cars coming out in the next several years will undoubtedly be different and less innovative than the versions that come out in ten years hence, and so on.

Framework Overall

For those of you that want to learn about self-driving cars, you can potentially pick a particular element and become specialized in that aspect. Some engineers are focusing on the sensory devices. Some engineers focus on the controls activation. And so on. There are specialties in each of the elements.

Researchers are likewise specializing in various aspects. For example, there are researchers that are using Deep Learning to see how best it can be used for sensor fusion. There are other researchers that are using Deep Learning to derive good System Action Plans. Some are studying how to develop AI for the Strategic aspects of the driving task, while others are focused on the Tactical aspects.

A well-prepared all-around software developer that is involved in self-driving cars should be familiar with all of the elements, at least to the degree that they know what each element does. This is important since whatever piece of the pie that the software developer works on, they need to be knowledgeable about what the other elements are doing.

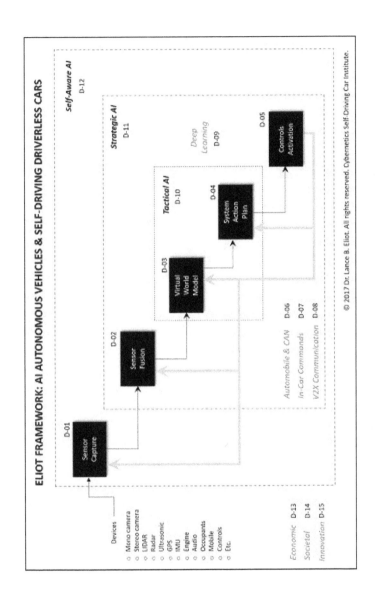

ELIOT FRAMEWORK: AI AUTONOMOUS VEHICLES & SELF-DRIVING DRIVERLESS CARS

Self-Aware AI D-12

Strategic AI D-11

Tactical AI D-10

Deep Learning D-09

Sensor Capture D-01

Sensor Fusion D-02

Virtual World Model D-03

System Action Plan D-04

Controls Activation D-05

Devices
o Mono camera
o Stereo camera
o LIDAR
o Radar
o Ultrasonic
o GPS
o IMU
o Engine
o Audio
o Occupants
o Mobile
o Controls
o Etc.

Automobile & CAN D-06
In-Car Commands D-07
V2X Communication D-08

Economic D-13
Societal D-14
Innovation D-15

© 2017 Dr. Lance B. Eliot. All rights reserved. Cybernetics Self-Driving Car Institute.

CHAPTER 2

TRIUNE BRAIN THEORY
AND
AI SELF-DRIVING CARS

CHAPTER 2

TRIUNE BRAIN THEORY
AND AI SELF-DRIVING CARS

When I was a youngster, some of my playmates would hurl a verbal insult at one other by saying that the person was a lizard brain. Hey, you, yes you, the dolt standing there on the basketball court in the way of our playing a game, get you and your dimwitted lizard brain off the darned court, they would yell out. I don't believe that the same taunt of being referred to as a lizard brain is used much anymore and it has ultimately gone by the wayside as a handy retort for kids.

Lizard brain was a power-packed quick-response insult that could be used in a wide variety of circumstances. If you wanted to upscale the wording, you could instead say that someone had a reptilian brain. A less potent version would be to say that someone had a primitive brain, though the word "primitive" does not have much panache and lacks a gutsy zest or spirit to it. Overall, the implication of any of the variations of lizard brain was that you were presumably as dumb as a lizard, which, I suppose we could argue at length about whether lizards should so readily be categorized as dumb and it might be a somewhat unfair form of bias or prejudice.

There was a kind of scientific revival of referring to a lizard or reptilian brain in the 1990's when a book by Paul MacLean came out, known today as a now-classic entitled "The Triune Brain in Evolution." His research had been going on for many years and he had been gradually formulating his theory of the human brain, namely that it consists of three major portions, thusly referred to as the triune brain. For those of you that enjoy words, triune is a fancy way of saying that you have something that consists of three things in one.

The triune brain theory postulates that the human brain physically evolved over time and consists of three separate parts. Presumably, evolution of the brain over time coincides with the rise of humanity and the bolstering of our thinking processes.

The three parts are united in that they ultimately work together in various fashions to undertake human thinking. Though there is a united aspect, they are nonetheless considered distinctive in their own right each.

Furthermore, the triune perspective suggests that it is feasible and reasonable to ascribe particular kinds of thinking-related functionality to each of the three parts.

This notion of having three separable and distinct functions might be likened to certain aspects of a car. If I had a car engine in front of us, I might tell you that one part has to do with the generating of thrust that is used to propel the car, and there is also a part or segment for keeping the engine cool by the use of liquid or air, and a third part or potion that lubricates the engine. That's a triune.

We all would agree that those three elements or portions of the engine are necessary to achieve full and appropriate use of the engine. I say this because we could pretend that we might eliminate any of the three, and we'd end-up with problems, I dare assert. Get rid of the cooling system and pretty quickly the engine will overheat and likely seize up. If you had the cooling system and the lubrication, but took out the engine thrust portion, you wouldn't be getting anywhere soon. And so on.

In the case of the triune brain theory, the three proposed portions are named as follows:

- Reptilian portion (also known as the Lizard Brain)
- Paleomammalian portion (also known as the Limbic System)
- Neomammalian portion (also known as the so-called Thinking Brain)

I've already introduced to you the Reptilian portion by mentioning that it used to be an insulting reference to suggest that a human being has a reptilian or lizard brain. In the triune theory, this portion of the brain has to do with your instincts. It includes brain elements that are often described as the brainstem and the striatum (also known as the basal ganglia or nuclei). In a manner of speaking, you could say it is the "blockhead" part of the brain that does the simplest and least thoughtful kinds of thinking efforts.

For example, you are in the woods and see an angry bear. Your first instinctive reaction is to use the much-valued fight-or-flight response. You will either immediately start to hightail it out of there and hope that you can outrun the bear, or you might instead opt to stand your ground and take on the bear in a one-on-one battle royale. There's a moment of first reaction in which you aren't "thinking" thoughtfully about those two options. In nearly one instantaneous split second, your feet start to run, and you go along, or you put up your dukes and wait to see how angry this bear really is.

Presumably, the fight-or-flight response is being undertaken by the Reptilian portion of your brain. It has your core instinctive capabilities. The basics of survival are burned into that Lizardry segment. It tends to operate very fast. There isn't much processing presumably taking place. The reptile-like reflex is a handy tool in your brain since it can kick into gear immediately and spur your body into similarly quick reactions.

Let's now consider the second portion of the triune brain.

The paleomammalian portion of your brain is said to consist of higher levels of thinking capabilities, including your emotions, your overall memory storage and access, your behavioral fundamentals such as parenting behavior and reproductive behavior. I had mentioned earlier that the triune theory postulates that our brain evolved over time and as such, this paleomammalian portion is considered the next step up in a mammalian evolution, beyond the Reptilian portion.

Okay, let's get back to the vexing and dangerous moment of standing in front of an angry bear. Suppose your Reptilian portion had started your body to run away from the bear. On the heels of that action (pun!), the paleomammalian portion might begin to emerge in your mind, adding some thinking aspects about the bear. Maybe you begin to contemplate that the bear could catch-up with you and it scares the heck out of you. Your mind now races with the emotions of the moment. Up until the paleomammalian portion getting into the matter, you were going solely on instincts. Now, the emotional roller coaster kicks into gear.

Let's add the third portion of the triune into the matter, the neomammalian portion.

The neomammalian segment of your brain is the higher-level thinking element of your mind. With this portion, you are able to think in abstract ways, you can communicate using language, you can mentally craft plans and carry them out. From an evolutionary perspective, this third portion of the brain came along after the other two. It is what makes us apparently differentiable from animals in that it gives us the brain superpower of being able to think in lofty terms, composing Shakespeare, designing rockets to get us to the moon, and being able to make sense of E=MC squared.

In the case of the angry bear, the neomammalian portion might get involved and identify that running away is not going to be very effective since there is a sheer cliff in the only direction that you can run. This might then have the neomammalian portion concoct a plan of having you climb a tree instead and try to get out of the reach of the bear, and perhaps be able to kick at the bear if it tries to climb the tree too.

All three portions are now chiming in about the bear situation. It's hard to say which of the three portions will necessarily prevail in this setting.

The Reptilian portion might be overriding any of the rest of your mind and forcing you to act on instinct. It could be that the paleomammalian rush of emotions is going to cloud the Reptilian instincts, and meanwhile the neomammalian portion intercedes and tells them both to put aside their noisy efforts and let it solve the problem at-hand.

When I mentioned that the triune theory postulates that the three portions are united, I was not stating that they are always in agreement. They might be diametrically opposed to each other. The angry bear circumstance can be used to highlight this kind of tension between each of the three portions. You've likely spoken with people that told you they reacted in a situation out of instinct, though they believed that the rest of their mind was arguing for an alternative approach to solving the crisis.

At any point in time, any of the three portions might prevail in terms of shaping your thinking and your efforts. There can be a lack of balance in the sense that one prevails, or two prevail, over the other portion or portions.

They could also all three be perfectly aligned.

Suppose the Reptilian portion indicated stand and fight that imposing bear, and the Paleomammalian was infusing you with a fierce sense of protecting your own child (we'll add that your son or daughter is standing there with you), and the Neomammalian portion analyzed the numerous avenues of stay or escape and concluded that challenging the bear was the right thing to do. All three portions happen to be in agreement.

I'm sure you seen people say that they hear voices in their head. Assuming that you aren't mentally deranged, it could be that you are somehow able to sense or realize the debate among the three portions of your triune brain.

Be aware though that there are some that say you cannot really "know" what your brain is doing and that any belief that you sensed an internal debate of the triune is completely made-up by you. It is perhaps your neomammalian portion is preparing a nifty story about what your brain is doing and has nothing to do with what is actually occurring in your brain. At some point, you might have been told that your brain has the three portions and that they can argue, so your neomammalian "thinking" portion has grabbed hold of that idea and gets you to believe that you can introspectively sense your mental processes.

This then brings us too to the matter of whether you buy into the triune brain theory.

Some would say that the theory was handy at the time that it was being proposed. It helped us to get our hands around the vast complexities of the human brain. It sparked discussion and research into the biologically mechanical and chemical inner workings of the brain. For a slew of good reasons, the theory was helpful.

There are now some that argue the triune brain theory is a grossly oversimplified way of modeling the brain. As such, they tend to say that we need to depart from the triune theory. If we remain wedded to the triune theory, we'll merely continue to chip away at trying to figure out these three parts of the brain. It will constrain how we approach analyzing the brain and the thinking that arises from our brain.

Maybe there are really five major portions of the brain. If so, we are incorrectly and artificially imposing a three-portion model onto something that really consists of five portions. This means that ultimately our three-portion model will need to come apart if we are going to make true further progress. Meanwhile, those clinging to the three-portion model might be missing the bigger picture and might be holding back the discovery of the five major portions.

Let's also consider that the five portions aren't necessarily just arrived at by adding two portions to the three that have already been delineated. Maybe we need to completely recast the original three portions. Toss aside the three portions to free your model to be whatever it is to be and start anew to come up with the five major portions.

On the oversimplification criticism, it might also be oversimplified to postulate that there are only say three to five major portions. Perhaps there are a dozen. Maybe there are a hundred major portions. Why does the brain need to be only a small number of major portions? That's just a means to make things simpler for us to grasp what it is, but this doesn't necessarily need to be the reality of how the brain actually is structured.

Besides the rather simplistic appeal of the triune theory as a kind of threepeat, it also has an added allure that it claims the three portions are based on evolution. This provides an added punch to bolster the theory because it offers a basis for why the three exist and how they came to be. Any competing theory is going to have to somehow contend with the evolution strengthening associated with the triune theory.

Allow me to explain. If you come up with a competing theory that says the brain has five major portions, it will right away be questioned as to how or why the brain has five major portions. What is the cause for this structure? What justifies it?

In the triune theory, we get the nicely with-a-bow-wrapped aspect that the three each evolved over time. They progressively got us toward greater and greater levels of thinking. Each portion has its own set of thinking-like elements. Furthermore, there are lots of other things in life that we ascribe to threes, and so the three portions of the brain are quite a nice fit to our overarching human-led believes about the magic of the number three.

Those multiple layers of neatly packaged justification for the triune brain theory are what makes it so compelling and enduring. It is also what makes it hard to dispel. You have to undermine the evolutionary aspects to undercut its rationalization as a theory. You have to argue that the separability of the mental functions is not true in terms of what the brain actually does.

So, which is it, does the triune brain theory provide us with a rich map to guide our efforts to dig into the brain and figure out what makes us think and what makes us tick, or does the theory potentially hamper our efforts and put a constraint around how we maybe should be studying the brain. The model could be shackling our efforts and we regrettably don't realize that's the case.

If you examine the "evolution" of the triune brain theory, much of it arises from research in comparative neuroanatomy.

In this case, I am referring to how the triune brain theory itself was formulated and offer insight that might be used to both explain triune brain theory and perhaps ultimately be an avenue that either reinforces it or might ultimately challenge and undermine it.

Comparative neuroanatomy is an approach to studying the brain that says we might be able to figure out the human brain by comparing it to the brains of other animals.

By doing a comparison and a contrasting of human brains versus animal brains, we can perhaps discover what we have that they don't, and this added piece might be the final piece in the puzzle that makes us thinker and humans. Note that there might also be brain portions that animals have that we don't have, and for which perhaps those are pieces that we once jettisoned and doing so aided our emergence of human intelligence. It is important to consider the full range of comparison and contrasting. Don't throw anything out along the way.

Researchers that undertake comparative neuroanatomy typically look quite closely at physical brains. What is the size of a human brain? What is the size of a mouse brain? What is the size of a monkey brain?

They also look at the structures of the brain. How many neurons does each type of brain have? How many synapses? How do they seem to be intertwined?

There is the black box approach too. Rather than trying to carve apart brains like you do turkeys at a Thanksgiving dinner, maybe focus on the behaviors that result from having brains. What kinds of thinking and solving of problems can a human brain accomplish? What about for mice? What about for monkeys?

This now takes us into the realm of Artificial Intelligence (AI).

One of the most vocal debates about trying to create automation that exhibits intelligent behavior is whether you need to first know how the human brain physically works, or whether you can skip that aspect and just aim at the behaviors that emerge out of thinking humans.

The triune brain theory attempts to cover both the physical inner workings of the brain and also commingle that with the resulting thinking behaviors that arise from the brain. Some might say you aren't going to get to unlock both. Trying to get both the inner aspects and the outer aspects figured out might be too much. You are biting off more than you can chew.

As such, some say that for AI, it could be that trying to crack the inner code of the brain structure and how it works, well, we might not ever figure that out. Or, it might take eons to figure it out. Thus, if you are predicating achieving true AI based on the nut cracking of the human brain, forget it since the brain will remain an enigma for a very long time. You are on a fool's errand if you are putting first the need to decipher the brain, some say.

Those that say we should aim to achieve the end-results of thinking and not care how it arises in the brain, they too are readily criticized. Some would say they are failing to leverage that which we have all around us and readily at our fingertips for studying, namely the human brain.

If you are not going to use the brain as your basis to arrive at intelligence, you are then presumably having to find a means that otherwise does not exist, or you are accused of somewhat blindly trying to retrace the evolutionary cycle that took thousands upon thousands upon thousands of years to "figure" out how to arrive at intelligence.

Darned if you do, darned if you don't.

For those that are developing Deep Learning systems and using artificial neural networks, particularly the use of deep or large-scale neural networks, it might be suggested they are trying to go the route of the inner workings of the brain. They seem to assume that if you amass enough of the linchpins of what the brain seems to be composed of, voila there will be intelligence that emerges from the spaghetti.

There are critics though that say the use of artificial neural networks is not particularly based on the real-world aspects of what we know or have yet to discover about the rudimentary wiring of the brain. It might seem like it, from a surface or simplification basis, but otherwise it is not at all the same thing. It is a mathematical simplification, some say an oversimplification.

Furthermore, there are some that assert we are not doing enough of a "comparative neuroanatomy" within the realm of artificial neural networks. Generally, nearly all of the neural networks being done on a large-scale basis are not being done in a manner that allows a comparison and contrasting between them. Each is its own one-off. Each is often hidden from other researchers and not revealed so that others can see what it is composed of.

In the case of a human brain, a mouse brain, and a monkey brain, you can relatively readily dig into those brains and try to compare and contrast them. Sure, you might argue that many of the factors being used to compare and contrast might not have much to do with how intelligence arises in brains. We might be using metrics that aren't correlated to intelligence and therefore those measures or metrics could be misleading.

But at least the comparisons and contrasts can be made. The same cannot be as readily stated about the large-scale or deep artificial neural networks.

What does this have to do with AI self-driving cars?

At the Cybernetic AI Self-Driving Car Institute, we are developing AI software for self-driving cars. One interesting aspect involves whether the triune brain theory can be applied to the AI systems being developed for AI self-driving cars. We believe so.

Allow me to elaborate.

I'd like to first clarify and introduce the notion that there are varying levels of AI self-driving cars. The topmost level is considered Level 5. A Level 5 self-driving car is one that is being driven by the AI and there is no human driver involved. For the design of Level 5 self-driving cars, the auto makers are even removing the gas pedal, brake pedal, and steering wheel, since those are contraptions used by human drivers. The Level 5 self-driving car is not being driven by a human and nor is there an expectation that a human driver will be present in the self-driving car. It's all on the shoulders of the AI to drive the car.

For self-driving cars less than a Level 5, there must be a human driver present in the car. The human driver is currently considered the responsible party for the acts of the car. The AI and the human driver are co-sharing the driving task. In spite of this co-sharing, the human is supposed to remain fully immersed into the driving task and be ready at all times to perform the driving task. I've repeatedly warned about the dangers of this co-sharing arrangement and predicted it will produce many untoward results.

Let's focus herein on the true Level 5 self-driving car. Much of the comments apply to the less than Level 5 self-driving cars too, but the fully autonomous AI self-driving car will receive the most attention in this discussion.

Here's the usual steps involved in the AI driving task:
- Sensor data collection and interpretation
- Sensor fusion
- Virtual world model updating
- AI action planning
- Car controls command issuance

Another key aspect of AI self-driving cars is that they will be driving on our roadways in the midst of human driven cars too. There are some pundits of AI self-driving cars that continually refer to a utopian world in which there are only AI self-driving cars on the public roads. Currently there are about 250+ million conventional cars in the United States alone, and those cars are not going to magically disappear or become true Level 5 AI self-driving cars overnight.

Indeed, the use of human driven cars will last for many years, likely many decades, and the advent of AI self-driving cars will occur while there are still human driven cars on the roads. This is a crucial point since this means that the AI of self-driving cars needs to be able to contend with not just other AI self-driving cars, but also contend with human driven cars. It is easy to envision a simplistic and rather unrealistic world in which all AI self-driving cars are politely interacting with each other and being civil about roadway interactions. That's not what is going to be happening for the foreseeable future. AI self-driving cars and human driven cars will need to be able to cope with each other.

Returning to the topic of the triune brain theory, let's consider how this relates to AI and the advent of AI self-driving cars.

The first aspect involves whether the AI of self-driving cars should be based on a primarily brain-based underlying structure, vis-à-vis Deep Learning and large-scale neural networks, or whether it should be based on a symbolistic approach of focusing on artificial intelligence that is exhibited in human driving behavior.

I earlier described that there is an ongoing and vocal debate about which of those two approaches is the sounder and more likely to get us toward true AI.

Currently, other than the use of Deep Learning and deep neural networks in the sensory data portion of an AI self-driving car, there is actually not a significant amount of the AI in an AI self-driving car that is shaped around the notion of a brain-based kind of structure. For now, the prevailing Version 1.0 of AI self-driving cars is going to be based on a more programmatic construct, and we'll have to wait and see how well this pans out, plus it could be that the Version 2.0 of AI self-driving cars swings further into the brain-based kind of structures, especially as that neural network style approach further evolves to become more robust.

The second aspect to consider is the notion of comparative neuroanatomy. I had earlier mentioned that there is relatively scant comparison and contrasting going on in the development of Deep Learning and large-scale neural networks. Developments tend to be proprietary and not provided for wide open analyses and comparisons.

The same kind of proprietary and shall we say secretive approach is being used by the auto makers and the tech firms that are crafting the AI for self-driving cars. There is no readily available means to do any kind of comparison or contrasting of the numerous underway AI self-driving car efforts, other than to try and examine any outward metrics such as number of miles driven and number of disengagements, though these are woeful metrics for doing any under-the-hood assessments and comparisons.

This is not to suggest that they are somehow wrong to be so secretive. The investment costs in developing the AI for self-driving cars is enormous and each of the auto makers and tech firms is hopeful of recouping those costs by the revenues they'll derive once their creations are functioning.

It is assumed by many that the first to the trough of self-driving cars is going to capture the market, a treasure trove awaits, and so why should any of these firms be willing to widely share their expensive secret sauce? It doesn't make much dollars-and-sense to do so. It could also jeopardize each respective efforts to cross the finish line first.

Others contend that if AI self-driving cars begin to get into various car accidents, there is a chance that the government will step harder into the fray. This could potentially include forcing the auto makers and tech firms to make available the inner guts of their AI systems, doing so to grapple with what might be a perceived lack of attention to safety aspects.

This aiming to open the kimono might also be undertaken via lawsuits brought against the auto makers and tech firms. If AI self-driving cars do get into various car accidents, you can bet that lawyers will be bringing a slew of lawsuits and will argue that too little was done on safety. To some degree, this will bring the inner portions of the AI systems into the courtroom and into the spotlight.

Let's shift our attention now toward the triune brain theory and its claim of three major portions of the human brain.

Recall, it is three portions, each separate, yet also united in their efforts, and are presumably based on evolution over time, encompassing becoming more elevated in terms of increasing levels of thinking capabilities.

As far as I know, there aren't any similar triune type of efforts underway by the auto makers or tech firms in terms of how they have opted to organize or structure their AI systems for their self-driving cars. In that sense, there isn't the use of a "three major portions" to the AI systems of self-driving cars.

If you were to macroscopically look at their AI systems for their self-driving cars, my framework that I earlier mentioned would be closer to the notion of dividing up separate portions that work in a united fashion, including for example a sensor data collection and interpretation, a sensor fusion, a virtual model updating, an AI action planning, and a car controls command issuance portions. This involves at least five major system portions, though there are many more and my framework depicts those further.

Overall, I don't believe we've gotten the AI systems of self-driving cars to fall into a rut by deciding to try and stick to some three-major portions notion. That's the good news.

The not so good news is that some of the AI systems of self-driving cars are overly complex. They are not well structured. They are not well organized. Their existing structure and organization is more akin to being byzantine than it is to being carefully and systematic composed. That's worrisome.

You might be wondering how such a modern-day AI system could be anything but perfectly well structured. The answer is that most of these AI systems have been rapidly evolving, partially due to the race to see who gets to the moon first. Pressures to push forward on getting the AI up-and-going are so tremendous that it is difficult to be mindful of how you are putting things together.

There's a famous line among software engineers in AI self-driving cars, namely that there isn't any style when you are in a knife fight. Caring about style is way down on the list when you are dealing with pure survival issues and the knife fight is earnestly underway. That's what is happening in the AI self-driving car arena. It might not seem like a knife fight to those on the outskirts of the industry but be aware that within the industry it is a fierce and ongoing take-no-prisoners environment.

The point being that rather than being overly constrained to a limited set of major systems or subsystems, and then hanging everything else off of those structures, there tends to be a more organic and sprawling structure to the AI systems of many self-driving cars underway.

With this kind of sprawl, there is a heightened chance of hidden bugs and errors. There is a much hard time involved in rooting out problems. Likewise trying to include safety, or perhaps retrofitting safety, becomes problematic. I am pretty sure that once AI self-driving car accidents begin to occur, and when the heat is turned on by the lawsuits and potential regulatory action, the laying bare of some of these AI systems is going to be ugly.

Let's consider another element of the triune brain theory and see how it applies to AI self-driving cars. One crucial aspect is that the three major portions of the brain are separate and yet united. They work together, though this does not mean they necessarily get along. The case of the angry bear helped to illustrate that the three portions might have quite different reactions to the same situation.

This is definitely an aspect to be wary about the AI systems of self-driving cars. With the perhaps overly complex nature of the AI systems and subsystems in a self-driving car, in theory they are working separately and yet are united. The united aspect tends to be shaped around a centralized controller.

Sadly, there are some AI developers and AI self-driving cars that have not yet vetted the numerous points of contention between the complex sprawl of AI systems and subsystems in their self-driving car.

This means that you might have an image processing portion that examines a camera image or video stream in real-time and determines that the road ahead is clear, and meanwhile the radar processing portion determines that there might be a truck or similar large object crossing the road ahead of the in-motion self-driving car. Some believe this might have been a factor for example in the real-world case of the Tesla in Florida that ended-up in a deadly crash.

These kinds of internal AI systems and subsystems contentions are akin to reacting to the angry bear in my story earlier. Which of the competing "viewpoints" about what is ahead should prevail when the AI action planner has to decide whether to continue the car unabated forward or maybe do an emergency stop?

If you begin to calculate the number of AI subsystems and systems in a self-driving car, and multiply in such a manner to consider the number of potential internal contentions, it becomes clear that unless the AI developers are being quite meticulous about their building of contingencies, at some point a loophole is going to be reached. The loophole might arise once in a blue moon, but when you are dealing with a multi-ton car that is going at 65 miles per hour, blue moons are going to be costly in terms of the potential of human injuries or deaths.

Another interesting aspect of the triune brain theory consists of the notion that the Reptilian portion is likely to react more quickly than the other portions. It's the gut instinctive reaction mechanism.

This can be welcomed when you are faced with a rapidly emerging situation for which there might not be time to think things through. Merely reacting upon impulse might be the difference between making it out of a dire situation versus not.

Upon seeing an angry bear, the split seconds involved in allowing the neomammalian portion (the Thinking Brain) to ponder what to do, it could be that the bear has time to grab you and your options are now narrowed, such as you no longer have the opportunity to run away.

Meanwhile, the Reptilian or Lizard Brain could maybe have saved you, doing so by acting instinctively. Of course, the Reptilian portion could also cause your death, since the instinct might be to fight the bear, while the thinking brain might have realized that fighting the bear was a no-chance solution. There are tradeoffs in terms of the which of the portions might prevail.

But the essence on this point is that the Reptilian portion is suggested as being the fastest of the three portions of the brain.

We can leverage that notion into the design of AI self-driving cars.

One of the biggest issues confronting an AI self-driving is the time factor. The AI system must be continually watching the clock.

A car that's in-motion at 65 miles per hour has a limited amount of time to decide what action to take. The AI cannot meander or ponder excessively a myriad of options. Indeed, similar to the angry bear, if the AI is in the midst of determining that it could escape getting hit from behind by another car, doing so by slipping into a small gap between two cars to the right of the self-driving car, it could be that by the time the AI decides to move into the gap, the gap has dissipated because the cars in the other lane have moved forward.

With the self-driving car in-motion and when complicated by other nearby cars also in motion, the timing of figuring out what to do must be relatively fast. Options as to maneuvers of the self-driving car will only be possible in short windows of time. The longer the AI goes to try and identify what to do, the odds are that the number of available and viable avenues of safety are going to be reduced.

I refer to this timing matter as the "cognition timing" of the AI self-driving car. This is a real-time system and therefore must be battling the clock at every moment. When the Uber self-driving car incident occurred in Phoenix, I had right away predicted that it might be partially due to an internal timing aspect, and it turns out that I was right. Time is king in an AI system and subsystems of a self-driving car.

Pulling together then the triune brain theory model with the need for fast processing by the AI of a self-driving car, we are advocates of an approach of having a kind of Reptilian portion of the AI system for a self-driving car.

Here's what we mean by this Reptilian metaphor.

There should be a core aspect of the overall AI system that acts like an instinctive portion. It is relatively stripped down in comparison to the full-blown and likely overly complex entire AI system and subsystems of the self-driving car. This tightly woven and smaller core is the last-man-standing if the clock has run out of time and something needs to be done.

The overarching AI system might get itself tied into a knot and not be able to pull out its head in time to realize that something must be done about the control of the self-driving car. In a circumstance whereby the self-driving car has gotten into a dire situation, the default of inaction because the AI overall system has gotten itself bogged down would seem undesirable as an approach.

In lieu of the overarching AI being able to proceed, the core or instinctive portion would step into the matter. Due to being stripped down, it is built and has been tested to be fast, very fast. As needed, it would issue car controls commands of a fundamental nature to try and save the day.

I'd like to emphasize that this is a last-resort option. The core is simplistic. It does not have the means to make the more robust kinds of decisions that the fuller AI system and its array of subsystems does. The instinctive choices it makes can be the wrong choices. We're focusing herein on the difference between making no choice, assuming that the fuller AI has not been able to reach a conclusion of what to do, and making some choice, though albeit one that is off-the-cuff.

For some AI developers, this idea that there would be a stripped-down Reptilian-like core that could make any decisions and issue cars control commands is horrifying and entirely out-of-the-question. No way, they would say. You cannot drop down to an instinct for driving of a car. Abysmal!

I would certainly and wholeheartedly agree that it is quite unappetizing.

If you can instead guarantee that the fuller AI system will never get into a bogged down state, of which it is unable to make a needed decision in time (suggesting that no car control commands will be issued and whatever the self-driving car is doing will continue by default), and the AI overarching system is so solid assuming that this absolutely will not ever happen, the Reptilian-like core is most certainly not needed. Scrap the Reptilian, in that case.

I have serious doubts that anyone can reasonably issue such a guarantee.

Therefore, the Reptilian gets back onto the table as a last-resort option.

Of course, this is not so easy to build and nor to invoke.

What portion of the AI system and subsystems will decide that the Reptilian core should be invoked? It could be a Catch-22. The overall AI system is so hopelessly engrained in what it is doing that it fails to realize the clock is out-of-time and therefore fails to hand the reins over to the Reptilian core. In that case, the Reptilian was there, but not invoked, and it is a sad day that the very contingency put in place had no chance to kick into gear.

If you say that the Reptilian-core can invoke itself, which presumably is how the triune brain theory postulates that things happen, we are then faced with a different kind of problem. Let's suppose the neomammalian portion of the AI system is doing its thinking thing, and the Reptilian-core will activate when say the clock is reaching a preset time threshold of a countdown.

Okay, so the overarching AI system is trying to consider a myriad of options and examining the sensory data and the rest. The time threshold is reached. The Reptilian-core leaps to life. It does a rapid analysis and decides that the brakes should be stomped upon, doing so by immediately issuing a full-stop command to the braking system of the car.

It could be that the Reptilian just saved the human occupants in the self-driving car. The self-driving car comes to a screeching halt. It was about to ram into a stopped car that is full of humans that are on their way to a baseball game. Those humans are also saved by the instinctive Reptilian.

Not wanting to mislead you into believing the Reptilian will always be right, let's reconsider the scenario and assume that the Reptilian does decide to stomp on the brakes. Unfortunately, doing so causes the car behind the self-driving car to ram into the self-driving car. This kills the occupants of the self-driving car. It also kills the occupants in the ramming car. Oops. Bad choice by the Reptilian.

The real twist that I was trying to take you toward was the notion that it could be that the Reptilian gets invoked, due to the time threshold countdown, and while the Reptilian is deciding what to do, the neomammalian portion of the AI system and subsystem finishes figuring out what to do. The thinking portion says to push full throttle and accelerate out of the crisis. The Reptilian says to hit full brake and come to an immediate halt.

Yikes, these are diametrically opposed viewpoints!

We've already discussed that the same can happen in the triune brain theory model. Each of the three major portions of the brain are separate and can reach their own conclusions about what to do. They might not agree with each other. In your own brain, which of the three prevails? It is likely contextually determined rather than necessarily principled.

In any case, there would need to be a thoughtfully composed hand-off mechanism about when the Reptilian-core of the AI self-driving car is to be invoked, and what to do if during the live action of the Reptilian that the overarching AI system is ready to take back control.

This is generally true of any relatively complex real-time system and an issue at the forefront of properly done real-time designs.

Conclusion

The triune brain theory is fascinating and provides much food-for-thought about how we humans seem to be able to think. It has been a useful pair of glasses in which to see the world of the mind and attempt to investigate it.

The simplicity has wide appeal and makes the theory accessible to the public and to those steeped into the science of the brain.

There are those that have gradually come to believe that the triune model is oversimplified. This could undermine research by falsely portraying a structure that does not truly exist. Worse still, it might blind us from seeing the true structure, or constrain us from a willingness to explore and find the true structure.

As a metaphor for the design of AI systems, we can use the Reptilian portion as an indicator that there are going to be times at which a real-time AI system might need an instinctive core that is fast and streamlined. Going on instinct or guts is not risk free. In fact, it is likely much higher risk than using the other two portions of the triune brain, but if those portions aren't able to get the job done, it might be that instinct will rue the day.

What is also applicable about the triune brain theory is the basis of using comparative neuroanatomy.

It sure seems like it might be advantageous to try and do the same kind of comparisons and contrasts among large-scale Deep Learning neural networks. It could provide impetus for making greater progress on that front.

The next time that you are confronted with a personal crisis of some kind, perhaps you come upon an angry bear in the woods, try to see if you can sense your brain rattling around with thoughts about the situation, and whether it seems like those mental thoughts divide into the three major portions of the triune brain theory.

As a caveat, please don't stand there too long trying to do this introspection, since I'd prefer that you escape the angry bear first. Use your Reptilian portion, even if it means that someone might later call you a Lizard Brain. It would be worth it.

CHAPTER 3
CAR PARTS THEFTS
AND
AI SELF-DRIVING CARS

CHAPTER 3

CAR PARTS THEFTS
AND
AI SELF-DRIVING CARS

What do manhole covers, beer kegs, and catalytic converters have in common?

This seems like one of those crafty questions asked when interviewing for a job at a high-tech firm. It is admittedly a tricky question.

The answer is that they are items that at one point or another were being stolen in large numbers. For the manhole covers, there was a case last year in Massachusetts of a man that stole seven of them and had tried to sell them for scape metal at a salvage yard, and in some countries they are faced with a raft of such thefts. A few years ago, beer kegs were being stolen to the tune of 300,000 kegs a year, doing so to sell the kegs for about $50 each in steel scrap.

Currently, the United States is seeing a surge in thefts of catalytic converters. You might assume that the thieves are trying to sell the catalytic converter as a used part and hoping to get unsuspecting car repair shops and car owners to buy these "hot" devices as a replacement when an older one on your car is unworking or gets damaged in an accident. Nope. The thieves are seeking to grab the palladium that's in the catalytic converters.

Yes, palladium.

Palladium is a rare metal that is silvery and white in overall color. It is part of the Platinum Group Metals (PGM) and has the handy properties of a low melting point and being the least dense of the PGMs. From a humanity perspective, the palladium in a catalytic converter is essential as it converts around 90% of the noxious gases coming out of your car's exhaust into much less dangerous chemicals (generally producing carbon dioxide, nitrogen, and simple water vapor). Palladium is also used in fuel cells and when combined with oxygen and hydrogen is a nifty producer of electrical power, heat, and water.

As they say, palladium doesn't though grow on trees. You need to find it and mine it. Or, as the thieves would say, you need to remove it and steal it. Your catalytic converter is usually in the underbody of your car and sits between the exhaust pipe and the engine or your car. In Chicago, they have had thieves recently go along a block at the wee hours of the morning and one-by-one crawl underneath cars to remove and steal the catalytic converter. Another popular approach involves going into a parking lot such as at an airport and stealing the catalytic converters from the long-term parked cars.

Here's a bit of a shocker, the value of palladium is now worth more than gold. No need to give someone a gold watch or a gold necklace, instead they should be happier to get a palladium coated gift. It is estimated that the thieves are typically getting around $200 or perhaps $400 when selling the catalytic converter palladium, depending upon the condition and how many grams are contained in the device.

Is it difficult to steal a catalytic converter? Sadly, no. With just a few tools and a few minutes, you can seemingly readily take one. You crawl underneath the target car and do your handiwork. There are even online videos on YouTube that show how to do this!

Of course, you would not target just any car and instead would want to go after certain kinds of cars, such as ones that are easier to steal from, and that have larger amounts of palladium in the catalytic converter, and are located in an area where you would guess that you won't get caught during the theft effort.

There are tons of car parts thefts annually in the United States alone (literally, tons worth!). Some of the car parts are stolen to glean the elements within them. Some of the car parts are being taken to then supply the huge market for used car parts. Perhaps nearly 1 million car parts and car thefts are undertaken each year, though it is hard to know how many happen since the crime is not always consistently reported. If you are interested in some fascinating statistics about stolen car parts and stolen cars, the National Insurance Crime Bureau (NICB) provides online stats that are insightful on the matter.

In the case of stealing a car part and attempting to resale it, there is an entire black-market that supports such efforts. When you go into a car repair shop to get your car fixed, and they offer to put into your car a used part, it could very well be a stolen part that they use. The car repair shop is not necessarily in on the thievery. They might be buying the used parts from seemingly reputable sources. It turns out that the supply chain of car parts is quite muddled and there is a kind of ease with which stolen car parts can appear to be legitimate used parts.

Some believe that the emergence of blockchain might be a means to curtail such sneaky acts. The notion is that all car parts would be notated in a publicly available online log, accessed via the Internet, and by doing so it would make the history and linage of the car part readily available. Anyone could figure out the status of a car part by merely consulting the blockchain.

The motivation for stealing car parts is rather apparent when you think about it. Car parts are becoming increasingly expensive and therefore the profit to be made by selling a stolen car part is quite handsome.

If car parts were dirt cheap, it would be difficult to make much money off stealing them. People that own cars are continually in need of getting replacement car parts, due to the wear-and-tear of an existing car part or sometimes due to the car part getting wrecked by a car accident.

I remember one car that I used to own that seemed to fall apart one-car-part at a time. I took my car to a small car repair shop that did quick work and was never crowded. They replaced one part that had failed due to wear-and-tear. About a month later, another car part failed. Once again, I took in the car to have the part replaced. This kept happening, nearly each month, for a period of about 6 months. The car repair shop probably posted my name on their calendar in anticipation that I'd be there the next month and so on.

Admittedly, it was an older car that had not been given much attention to keeping it in shape. I had bought it used and knew that it was likely to someday start to come apart at the seams. Once the seams started coming undone, it was a tsunami of car parts failures and replacements. What a pain in the neck!

In any case, the car parts thieves are choosy about which cars they steal from and which car parts they try to steal. Cars that are well-sold and the most popular brands of cars tend to be the right choice for stealing car parts from, since there is a much larger market potential of the need for used parts. Another angle too is cars that tend to be involved in car accidents, which then are in need of replacement car parts.

It's a demand and supply phenomena. Parts being stolen are dictated generally by the demand exhibited via car repair shops, and in combination with the used parts marketplace and the underground marketplace.

The car part needs to have sufficient profit potential, thus the more expensive it is, the more attractive as a target to steal.

The car part needs to be relatively easy to steal. If it takes too long to steal it, or if the chances of getting caught are high, thieves are not going to take the risk as readily.

The car part needs to be small enough that a thief can readily cart it away and then transport it to whatever locale might be needed to dispense with it. If the car part is extremely heavy or bulky, it makes the stealing of it much harder and along with complicating a fast getaway with the car part.

The car part needs to be removable without excessive effort. If the thief needs a multitude of tools to try and extract the part, or if the part is welded into place, these are barriers to stealing it. Likewise, if there is a car alarm system that the car part will potentially setoff when stealing the car part, that's a no-no kind of car part to try and take.

I realize you might be thinking that it would be "better" for the car parts thieves to consider taking the entire car, rather than futzing around trying to take a particular car part itself. Certainly ,the stealing of the entire car would be more efficient since you would have all of the car parts now available. You could either try to sell the entire car intact, or instead take apart the parts and sell those individually.

This reminds me of the occasion when my sports car was stolen here in Los Angeles.

I was a university professor at the time. I had parked my car in one of the on-campus parking lots. There wasn't any faculty designated parking per se, and so I parked in the same parking structure as did the students, the administrators, and the other faculty. Each time that I parked on-campus, I would drive throughout each parking structure, trying to find an available parking spot. It was one of those hunts for a parking spot kind of games, though I sometimes cut it close to class starting time and got into a bit of a sweat about finding an available parking stall.

One day, I parked my car in the mid-morning, getting parked in plenty of time to teach my lunch time class. I was teaching classes throughout the day. I also was teaching an evening class. At about 9:30 p.m., I walked out to the parking structure to drive home. When I got to where my car was supposed to be parked, it wasn't there. What? My mind raced as I thought that perhaps I had parked on a different floor and was just confused about where my car was.

I went to each floor of the parking structure and searched stridently to find my car. After covering the entire parking structure, I concluded that my car was not there. Had I perhaps parked in a different on-campus parking structure that day? No. I knew I had not. Maybe my car had been towed for some reason, perhaps I had not displayed my faculty parking tag, or my car was sloppily parked and took up more than one parking space.

I dutifully went to the campus security office. Had they perchance towed my car? No, they said they did not do so. They asked me what I did at the campus. When I explained that I was a professor, the office clerk made a small smirk and called over one of the campus security officers. They said they would take me over to the parking structure in one of the campus security golf-like carts and the officer would help me find my car.

Sure enough, the campus security officer drove me to the parking structure and slowly drove on each floor and past each car. Is that your car, the security officer would ask? No, I said. In fact, I was getting quite upset that this effort of slowly driving through the parking structure was taking place. I already had looked and was unable to find my car. The campus security officer insisted we would need to continue the slow poke search.

After exhausting the parking structure's set of cars and not having seen mine, I thought that we could now start to discuss what to do about my apparently stolen car. I assumed that an all-out broadcast would take place to alert numerous police and highway patrol to be on the look for my car. Police helicopters would take to the skies to find my car. Squad cars would be peeling out of police stations, seeking to find my car. Okay, maybe I watch too many movies and TV shows, but I had in mind that my car was important and by-gosh somehow someone should be looking for it.

The campus security officer proceeded to drive us to another one of the parking structures. Yikes! I bitterly complained and said that this was an utter waste of time. He then explained to me that the reason they do this is that it was possible that I had merely gotten mentally mixed-up about where I had parked my car. He also indicated that when I said that I was a faculty member, the reason that the clerk had smirked, they routinely had faculty that would claim their car was gone, yet it was sitting safely in a parking structure where they had parked it earlier in the day.

They had over time gotten used to "genius" level professors that might be incredible researchers but were not able to do everyday tasks very well. These faculty were often forgetful of mundane aspects. Sure, they might be able to explain the intricacies of some arcane area of science or technology and could be steeped in grand theories. They though were at times not able to tie their own shoes and nor keep track of where they parked their car.

I endured an eternity as we drove to each of the numerous parking structures and slowly drove throughout each one. It was painful and I kept thinking that the thieves of my car were merely being handed more time to drive it further and further away. Did they target a faculty member's car, doing so because they knew that the campus security would waste time trying to find it while letting the clock tick for the escape plan of the thieves?

Anyway, it was not in any of the parking structures. The campus security officer took my back to the main security office and I filled-in paperwork. After doing the paperwork, they said that there wasn't anything else needed to be done. I was puzzled. Were the helicopters getting underway and the police squads rallying to find my car?

Turns out that there are many cars stolen each day in Los Angeles. I might think my car was the only one being stolen, plus it was my treasured sports car, having a great deal of personal sentiment associated with it, yet the reality was that there were lots of cars being stolen daily. Sigh.

Furthermore, the campus security officer explained that the local gangs had an initiation challenge to join their gang, consisting of stealing a car at the nearby university. The best guess was that my car had been stolen by a gang, they would joy ride in it, and then likely take it across the border to a chop shop. At the chop shop, my car would be gutted, and the car parts then put out for resale.

This news was disheartening.

One aspect too that they had asked me, adding to my frustration at the time, was whether I had left the keys in my car. Say what? No, I said, of course I didn't do so.

I found out then that incredibly there are a preponderance of stolen cars wherein the owner left the keys in the car. The key is often one of the fobs that has the super-duper security capabilities, which auto makers spent many millions of dollars perfecting. Turns out that last year, it is estimated that around 60% of all stolen cars in the United States were taken by the thief simply using the keys left inside the car.

For those of us that are technologists, it highlights how humans can undermine the best of technology by how they behave. In spite of the handshake security capabilities that took years to perfect and embody in a key fob, it turns out that a lot of people merely leave the fob sitting inside the car. A car thief does not need any special skills to steal such a car.

This is reminiscent of the "hacking" of people's online accounts or their PC's or their IoT devices. Many people use a password that is easily guessed. I'm sure you are as frustrated as me that many of the so-called hackings of people's accounts are not due to any shrewd computer hacker, but instead by the simplistic and mindless act of trying obvious passwords. I say this is frustrating because the news often portrays these thieves as some kind of computer geniuses, when it was in actuality that the humans owning the computer accounts were lazy or ill-informed about setting better passwords.

I tell the story of my car being stolen to point out that it was apparently more likely that it would be turned into a treasure trove of used car parts, rather than trying to sell the entire stolen car itself. This makes sense. Selling a stolen car is likely to be riskier and requires that someone come up with a larger bag of cash to acquire it. Yanking off the parts and selling those is less chancy.

Unbelievably, at times the value of the parts exceed the value of the car itself. In other words, the amount of money you can make by selling the stolen parts is going to be more than if you tried to sell the entire car. In that case, when you toss into the equation the troubles and risks involved in selling an intact stolen car, the notion of taking the car to a chop shop makes a lot of sense. Divide up the car and sell the parts, then find a place to discard or bury or destroy whatever might be leftover.

What does this have to do with AI self-driving cars?

At the Cybernetic AI Self-Driving Car Institute, we are developing AI software for self-driving cars. One question that I often get asked at industry conferences involves whether AI self-driving cars will be subject to the stolen car parts marketplace. I believe so.

Allow me to elaborate.

I'd like to first clarify and introduce the notion that there are varying levels of AI self-driving cars. The topmost level is considered Level 5. A Level 5 self-driving car is one that is being driven by the AI and there is no human driver involved. For the design of Level 5 self-driving cars, the auto makers are even removing the gas pedal, brake pedal, and steering wheel, since those are contraptions used by human drivers. The Level 5 self-driving car is not being driven by a human and nor is there an expectation that a human driver will be present in the self-driving car. It's all on the shoulders of the AI to drive the car.

For self-driving cars less than a Level 5, there must be a human driver present in the car. The human driver is currently considered the responsible party for the acts of the car. The AI and the human driver are co-sharing the driving task. In spite of this co-sharing, the human is supposed to remain fully immersed into the driving task and be ready at all times to perform the driving task. I've repeatedly warned about the dangers of this co-sharing arrangement and predicted it will produce many untoward results.

Let's focus herein on the true Level 5 self-driving car. Much of the comments apply to the less than Level 5 self-driving cars too, but the fully autonomous AI self-driving car will receive the most attention in this discussion.

Here's the usual steps involved in the AI driving task:

- Sensor data collection and interpretation
- Sensor fusion
- Virtual world model updating
- AI action planning
- Car controls command issuance

Another key aspect of AI self-driving cars is that they will be driving on our roadways in the midst of human driven cars too. There are some pundits of AI self-driving cars that continually refer to a utopian world in which there are only AI self-driving cars on the public roads. Currently there are about 250+ million conventional cars in the United States alone, and those cars are not going to magically disappear or become true Level 5 AI self-driving cars overnight.

Indeed, the use of human driven cars will last for many years, likely many decades, and the advent of AI self-driving cars will occur while there are still human driven cars on the roads. This is a crucial point since this means that the AI of self-driving cars needs to be able to contend with not just other AI self-driving cars, but also contend with human driven cars.

It is easy to envision a simplistic and rather unrealistic world in which all AI self-driving cars are politely interacting with each other and being civil about roadway interactions. That's not what is going to be happening for the foreseeable future. AI self-driving cars and human driven cars will need to be able to cope with each other.

Returning to the topic of stolen car parts, let's consider how this might apply to the advent of AI self-driving cars.

First, let's all agree that an AI self-driving car is still a car. This might seem obvious, but I assure you that a lot of people seem to think that when you add the AI aspects to a car that the car somehow transforms into a magical vehicle. It's a car.

I mention this so that it is perhaps apparent that the same aspects of car parts being stolen are going to apply to the conventional parts of a self-driving car. If there are AI self-driving cars that have catalytic converters, and if the price of palladium remains high, you can reasonably assume that car thieves might want to steal the catalytic converter from your AI self-driving car.

So, overall, yes, AI self-driving cars face the same dangers of car parts thievery as might be the case for conventional cars. There are some important caveats to consider.

I've mentioned earlier that I anticipate the volume of AI self-driving cars will be a gradual build-up of adoption, and we'll continue to have conventional cars during that same time period. This means that there might not be many AI self-driving cars on the roadway. Recall that an important aspect of being a targeted car for stolen parts is that the car itself is popular. The more cars of a particular brand in the marketplace, the more the number of used car parts that are needed.

In the case of AI self-driving cars, the number of AI self-driving cars might be so low for the initial adoption period that it is not as worthwhile to steal a car part from an AI self-driving car as it is to steal from a conventional car that has greater popularity.

The thieves tend to react based on marketplace demand. If there aren't many AI self-driving cars out and about, there's little incentive to steal parts from those cars.

In a similar form of logic, if the AI self-driving cars are not as readily around, they are a harder target to find and steal from. The nice thing about popular cars, from a car parts thievery perspective, would be that you can find those popular cars just about anywhere, parked along the street, parked in mall parking lots, and so on.

The relatively rarity of AI self-driving cars at the start, before there is a gradual shift toward AI self-driving cars and away from conventional cars, means that finding an AI self-driving car to steal parts from will be an arduous task. I'm not saying that it becomes impossible, and I am sure that if the thieves think it worthwhile, they could hunt down the locations of AI self-driving cars.

Another factor to consider about AI self-driving cars will be their likely use on a somewhat non-stop basis. The notion is that an AI self-driving car is more likely to be used in a ridesharing service and therefore will be used potentially around-the-clock. If you don't need to hire a human driver, you can keep the AI driving the car all of the time. The more time the self-driving car is underway, and assuming you can fill it with paying passengers, the more money you make from owning an AI self-driving car.

This brings up the fact that trying to get to a parked and motionless AI self-driving car might be harder than it seems at first glance. A conventional car is parked and motionless for most of its time on this earth. You park your conventional car in a mall, and it waits until you come back to use it. That's not going to be the case presumably for AI self-driving cars. A self-driving car is more likely roaming to find paying passengers, rather than being parked for hours at a time.

Thus, besides the likely lesser number of AI self-driving cars on the roadway versus conventional cars, during the early stages of adoption of AI self-driving cars, even once AI self-driving cars become prevalent, they are bound to be underway most of the time.

This makes stealing car parts problematic in that the car itself is a kind of moving target. Imagine trying to slide underneath an AI self-driving car that is slowly cruising the street and waiting to be hailed by a passenger, and somehow a thief extracts the catalytic converter – that's a real magic act.

You might be wondering how many of the existing being-tested varying-levels of AI self-driving cars are having their car parts stolen? None that I know of.

Does that undermine the notion that there will be car parts stolen from AI self-driving cars? No, it does not undermine the argument.

As already stated, when the number of cars of a particular brand or model are low, there is little interest in trying to steal their car parts. That's certainly the case right now with the low number of AI self-driving cars of one kind or another being trial run on roadways.

An even greater factor right now is that the AI self-driving cars that are being trial run have a quite devoted crew that keeps those AI self-driving cars in tiptop working order. Unlike a conventional car, these special testing AI self-driving cars are handled delicately and devotedly by assigned car mechanics and engineers.

These AI self-driving cars are kept parked in secure locations, and they are maintained to a meticulous threshold. The auto makers and tech firms do not want their existing tryouts of AI self-driving cars to be undermined due to parts that fail or wear out. These are spoiled cars, being provided with by-hand daily care.

A car parts thief is unlikely to find any of these AI self-driving cars, and if they did, it would be in a secure location that has a crew doting to the self-driving car when it is parked.

When an AI self-driving car is in-motion, the camera is functioning to undertake image and video stream captures and analyze the roadway around the AI self-driving car, along with the other sensors doing the same, such as the radar, the ultrasonic, the LIDAR, etc. Any car parts thief would likely get caught on camera, making their theft someone stupid, when attempting to steal from an underway AI self-driving car, though I suppose they could try to wear a mask and disguise themselves.

I've already pointed out that since the AI self-driving car will be in-motion most of the time, a masked thief still has little chance of stealing any of the car parts. Admittedly, once the AI self-driving car is parked and motionless, the sensors are often no longer being powered and used, which means that you could be possibly undetected when stealing parts from the car. This will be something important to consider once AI self-driving cars become prevalent.

It is anticipated that once there are a lot of AI self-driving cars in the marketplace, it might not be the case that they will all be cruising around all of the time. It is suggested that there might be special areas that the AI self-driving cars go to wait for being summoned. These staging areas would resemble parking lots. The idea is that rather than an AI self-driving car driving around endlessly, which might not be very efficient, they would sit in temporary staging areas and await a request to be used.

I mention this because few of the AI self-driving car pundits have realized that we might reach a kind of saturation point of AI self-driving cars prevalence. It is admittedly a long way off in the future.

Overall, the notion is that if there is a saturation level in a given locale, it might not be prudent to have an AI self-driving car driving around and around, waiting to be put to use. The endless driving is going to cause wear-and-tear on the self-driving car, plus it will be using up whatever fuel is used by the AI self-driving car. As such, we might reach a point where it makes sense to have the oversupply of AI self-driving cars be staged in a temporary area until summoned.

I suppose the staging area could be a place to try and steal car parts from those waiting AI self-driving cars. I'll guess that by the time we have such a prevalence of AI self-driving cars, those staging areas would be well-protected and well-monitored. Seems less likely an easy target for car parts thievery.

One aspect that will potentially make AI self-driving cars an attractive target would be the specialized components included onto the self-driving car for the AI driving purposes. An AI self-driving car has lots of really good cameras, it has numerous radar devices, it might have LIDAR, it will have ultrasonic devices, and so on. This is exciting, especially as a goldmine for car parts theft. I can imagine the car thieves already salivating at this.

These sensory devices are an ideal target for car parts theft. They tend to be expensive, which I had mentioned earlier that the value of a car part is a crucial attractor for car parts thievery. There are many of them on each AI self-driving car, making the car target-rich. They tend to be small in size, meaning that you can readily steal and transport them.

The question is whether these sensors can be readily removed from an AI self-driving car or not.

On the one hand, if the sensors are well-embedded and bolted or meshed into the car, it is going to make things harder for car parts thieves to steal those car parts. Unlike the ease of taking a catalytic converter, these sensors might be arduous to extract from the self-driving car. As mentioned earlier, the longer it takes to steal a car part and the more difficult it is to steal it, the less likely the car part is as a worth-stealing car part.

Some are suggesting that we'll have add-on kits that can convert a conventional car into becoming an AI self-driving car. If that's the case, this is a potential gift from heaven for the car parts thieves. Presumably, an add-on kit means that you simply augment the car with these added sensors, making them more vulnerable to being taken off the car too. Easy on, easy off. It's the easy off aspect that makes the car thieves happy.

This would also make the selling of the stolen car parts easier too. Imagine a thriving market of add-on kits for AI components of an AI self-driving car. A huge marketplace might develop. It will be hungry for these specialized car parts. The underground will work double-time to try and fulfill the demand.

I've already stated in my writings and presentations that I doubt the add-on approach is going to be viable for AI self-driving cars. By this claim, I am suggesting that there won't a mass consumer add-on market. There could though be a car dealer marketplace of doing this after-market effort, though I doubt that will be likely either.

Does the potential lack of an AI self-driving car parts add-on market imply that the sensors on an AI self-driving car will necessarily be difficult to remove? No, not necessarily.

Here's why.

For an auto maker trying to maintain AI self-driving cars, they've got to be considering that the life of the sensors is limited, and they will breakdown. When the sensors need to be replaced, if they are somehow hidden and embedded within the body of the self-driving car, it will make it harder and costlier to have those sensors replaced.

I realize that the auto makers might not care about this facet and are so focused on just producing a viable AI self-driving car that they don't care right now about the maintenance side of things. Plus, if you like conspiracy theories, you might say that it is perhaps better for the auto maker to make it arduous and costly to replace the sensors, thus guaranteeing a lucrative maintenance fee after selling the AI self-driving car.

In any case, it isn't yet clear as to whether it will be made easy or hard to remove the sensors from an AI self-driving car. This might differ by car maker and car model.

The same question can be asked about the computer processors in the AI self-driving car. AI self-driving cars will be choke full of likely expensive computer processors and computer memory. These expensive and small sized components would be another potential target for car parts theft. Will these processors be so deeply embedded that it precludes much chance of car part thievery, or will they be readily accessed for maintenance purposes and therefore more prone to being stolen? We'll need to wait and see.

One additional aspect to keep in mind will be advances in anti-theft technologies.

It could be that once we have any prevalence of AI self-driving cars that there will be new advances in car anti-theft systems and those devices will be included into AI self-driving cars. If so, it might make stealing car parts a near impossibility.

Imagine a scenario in which a thief attempts to carry out a car parts theft on an AI self-driving car. The AI might detect the effort. It could then honk the horn or take some other effort to bring attention to the car. It might also use it's Over The Air (OTA) capabilities, usually used for pushing updates and patches into the AI system remotely via the cloud, and contact the authorities electronically to report a car parts robbery in progress.

Another futuristic possibility is the use of the V2V (vehicle-to-vehicle) electronic communications that will be included into AI self-driving cars.

Normally, the V2V will be used for an AI self-driving car to share roadway info with another nearby AI self-driving car. Perhaps an AI self-driving car has detected debris in the road. It might relay this finding to other nearby AI self-driving cars. They can then each try to avoid hitting the debris, being able to proactively anticipate the debris due to the V2V warning provided.

Suppose one AI self-driving car notices that a thief is trying to steal the parts from another AI self-driving car.

The observing AI self-driving car might try to honk its horn or make a scene, or it might via OTA contact the authorities, or it might try to wake-up the AI self-driving car that is the victim, doing so via sending a V2V urgent message. Assuming that the AI self-driving car was "asleep" and parked, the V2V message could awaken it, and then the "victim" self-driving could sound an alert or possibly even try to drive away.

Conclusion

What do manhole covers, beer kegs, and AI self-driving car sensors have in common? Similar to my earlier having asked this question, it could be that the AI self-driving car sensors will be stolen, in some cases to make use of them for their scrap value, but more likely kept intact and sold as used parts.

This is unlikely to happen anytime soon. There are too few AI self-driving cars being tested and available as a target for car parts thievery. Plus, those AI self-driving cars being tested are kept securely parked and are well pampered. They would be difficult to reach for purposes of stealing car parts.

Will the sensors and other AI physical components be easy to steal or hard to steal? They are going to be attractive due to their expensive cost and small size. Auto makers and tech firms are not likely considering the matter right now of whether those parts are able to be stolen or not. Instead, right now it's mainly about getting them to work and produce a true AI self-driving car.

The marketplace for those devices will be slim until there is a prevalence of AI self-driving cars. Therefore, this is a low-chance risk for now. We'll have to wait and see what the future holds.

I can just imagine in the future coming out to my vaunted AI self-driving car, which I would proudly opt to park in my driveway, doing so as a showcase for the rest of the neighborhood, and suddenly realizing that it has been stripped of its parts. Many of the conventional car parts might be taken, along with the AI specialized car parts. Darn it, struck by car thieves a second time in my life. Will it never end? I'd hope that helicopters were dispatched immediately, along with police drones, and squad cars, all searching for my stolen AI self-driving car parts. Get those dastardly heathens!

CHAPTER 4
GOTO FAIL BUG
AND
AI SELF-DRIVING CARS

CHAPTER 4

GOTO FAIL BUG
AND AI SELF-DRIVING CARS

I'm guessing that you've likely heard or read the famous tale of the Dutch boy that plugged a hole in a leaking dam via his finger and was able to save the entire country by doing so. I used to read this fictional story to my children when they were quite young. They delighted in my reading of it, often asking me to read it over and over.

Though this is a well-known children's tale in the United States, you might be surprised to know that it is little noted by the Dutch and that the author of the story, Mary Mapes Dodge, had never visited the Netherlands until a while after having published the fictional account.

Furthermore, the story itself is actually a story-within-a-story, nearly akin to the movie *Inception* of a dream within a dream. And, the dam story is based on other similar fictional accounts that had been floating around for many years. Thus, the dam story-within-a-story was not purely of an original nature by Mary Dodge. Nonetheless, I think we can all agree that she aided in the dam story becoming widely popular all around the world and provided a version of it that still resonates with us all, even in modern day times.

The novel containing the story-within-a-story is entitled "Hans Brinker; or, the Silver Skates: A Story of Life in Holland" and was published in 1865. The Hans Brinker tale is a touching lesson about personal honor and the efforts of a 15-year old boy named Hans Brinker and consumes the bulk of the pages in the novel. Within the longer tale there is a rather short story entitled "The Hero of Haarlem" about an unnamed Dutch boy that holds back a dam from imploding by the use of his finger.

For those of you that are sticklers for accuracy, others confusedly sometimes refer to the unnamed Dutch boy as Hans Brinker, but we do not know for sure the name of the boy in the story-within-a-story, and so for those claiming that it is Hans Brinker, they are likely misremembering the novel or confounding the two stories. You can use that trivia for one-upmanship, if you like.

In any case, one aspect that puzzled my young children was how a hole so small that it could be plugged by a finger could potentially jeopardize the integrity of the entire dam. Rather astute of them to ask. I read them the story to impart a lesson of life that I had myself learned over the years, namely that sometimes the weakest link in the chain can undermine an entire system, and incredibly too the weakest link can be relatively small and surprisingly catastrophic in spite of its size.

I guess that's maybe two lessons rolled into one.

The first part is that the weakest link in a chain can become broken or severed and thus the whole chain no longer exists as a continuous chain.

By saying it is the weakest link, we're not necessarily saying its size, and it could be a link of the same size as the rest of the chain. It could be even a larger link or perhaps even the largest link of the chain. Or, it could be a smaller link or possibly the smallest sized link of the chain. The point being that by size alone, it is not of necessity the basis for why the link might be the weakest. There could be a myriad of other reasons why the link is subject to being considered "the weakest" and for which size might or might not particularly matter.

Another perhaps obvious corollary regarding the weakest link aspect is that it is just one link involved. That's what catches our attention and underlies the surprise about the notion. We might not be quite so taken aback if a multitude of links broke and therefore the chain itself came into ruin.

The aspect that only one link can achieve such an untoward end is the startling element. It showcases that you might have done a tremendous job of making all the other links hearty, and yet if you somehow ignored one link or failed to consider its weaknesses, the rest of your efforts could be utterly undermined by that one link that you missed or contained a hidden or mistaken fault.

The second part of the lesson learned involves the cascading impact and how severe it can be as a consequence of the weakest link giving way.

In the case of the tiny hole in the dam, presumably the water could rush through that hole and the build-up of pressure would tend to crack and undermine the dam at that initial weakest point. As the water pushes and pushes to get through it, the finger-sized hole is bound to grow and grow in size, until inextricably the hole becomes a gap, and the gap then becomes a breech, and the breech then leads to the entire dam crumbling and being overtaken by the madly and punishingly flowing water.

Could this happen? Well, you might find of interest that in 1953 there really was a hole in a dam in the Netherlands, though this one was about 15 meters in size (which, though obviously larger than the size of a finger, it is still relatively small in comparison to the size of the entire dam wall). Officials quickly sought to find a nearby ship, one that in this case was about 18 meters in size and opted to use it as a plug for the hole. Once they managed to get the ship into the hole as a stopgap, they then piled sand bags around the perimeter of the ship to help prevent any additional water from tearing further expansions into the dam wall. A real-life example of the Dutch boy story!

If you are still not convinced that a single weakest link could undermine a much larger overall system, I'd like to enchant you with the now-famous account of the so-called "goto fail goto fail" saga that played out in February 2014. This is a true story. I will share with you the gory details.

For those of you that were aware of the matter at the time, you might find some joy or some revulsion in revisiting the circumstance. I remember at the time that it was a huge story, not only spreading like wildfire among the computer elite but it also managed to get national and international headlines in the mass media of the time.

The crux of the story is that one line of code, a single "Go To" statement in a software routine, led to the undermining of a vital aspect of computer security entailing Apple related devices.

Herein, I assert that the one line of code is the equivalent to a tiny finger-sized hole in a dam. Via that one hole, a torrent of security guffaws could have flowed. Fortunately, as far as we know today, it was patched quickly enough that there was little known damage that resulted.

At the time, and still to this day, there were reverberations that this single "Go To" statement could have been so significant.

For those outside of the computer field, it seemed shocking. What, one line of code can be that crucial? For those within the computer field, there was for some a sense of embarrassment, namely that the incident laid bare the brittleness of computer programs and software, along with being an eye opener to the nature of software development.

I realize that there were pundits that said it was freakish and a one-of-a-kind, but at the time I concurred with those that said this is actually just the tip of the iceberg. Little do most people know or understand how software is often built on a house of cards. Depending upon how much actual care and attention you devote to your software efforts, which can be costly in terms of time, labor, and resources needed, you can make it hard to have a weakest link or you can make it relatively easy to have a weakest link.

All told, you cannot assume that all software developers and all software development efforts are undertaking the harder route of trying to either prevent weakest links or at least catch the weakest link when it breaks.

As such, as you walk and talk today, and are either interacting with various computer systems or reliant upon those computer systems, you have no immediate way to know whether there is or is not a weakest link ready to be encountered.

I think it is instructive to explore the infamous "Go To" line of code that created an uproar and see what we can potentially learn from it.

With the case of the Dutch boy and the dam, I've already mentioned an overarching lesson to be learned, involving the dangers of a weakest link. Beyond that lesson, I'll offer some thoughts on ways in which such finger-sized software holes can either be prevented or at least be detected and provide software developer lessons learned thereof.

Let's start with a simple contextual background about aspects of programming. I'll be doing so in reference to the programming language C, which was used in the case of the infamous "Go To" line snafu.

We only need to be concerned with two of the most fundamental constructs in programming in order to assess the problem of concern. Those two constructs are the IF statement and the GO TO statement. I'll walk you through the syntax of those statements, meaning that I will explain how they are formed akin to forming a sentence if you were trying to write a story, indicating the respective format and punctuation used.

For an IF statement, you use it to formulate a logical condition that you'd like to determine whether something is true or not. This is done by stating the word IF and then followed by the condition. The condition is housed within parentheses' so that we can easily distinguish it, of which there is a left parenthesis for the start of the conditional and a right parenthesis for the ending of the conditional.

After the condition of the IF statement, you can place another statement, which will be performed if the condition is ascertained to be of a true value. This statement that follows the condition won't be performed if the condition is evaluated to be of a false value. At the tail-end of the IF statement itself, there is a semi-colon used, similar to how you might put a period at the end of sentence when writing a paragraph and wanting to denote where each sentence ends.

Thus, we have this: IF (condition) statement;

Let's say that I set a variable called A to the value of 1, and I set the value of a variable called B to a value of 0. I want to setup an IF statement that seeks to discover whether the value of the variable A is 1, which if so then I want to set the value of B to be 3. Kind of a nonsense thing to do but it is just for illustrative purposes.

Here's my code:

```
A = 1;
B = 0;
IF ( A = 1 ) B=3;
```

When I have the computer run my above code, it would proceed to set A to 1, it would set B to zero, and it would assess the IF statement by determining whether A is equal to 1, which in this moment is indeed true, and so the value of B would be set to 3.

Let's change the code and see what would happen based on the change. The condition indicates to test whether A is equal to 1. I'd like to change that to a test of whether A is not equal to 1. In this programming language, we'll use the exclamation mark in front of the equal sign to signify the "not" aspects of the test, thus the use of "!=" means the test of being "not equal" of whatever is being tested.

Here's my new code:

```
A = 1;
B = 0;
IF ( A != 1 ) B=3;
```

The code starts once again by setting A to 1 and B to 0. In this changed version of my code, the condition asks whether A is not equal to 1. Since A is actually equal to 1, it would be false to say it is not equal to 1. Because the condition is assessed as being false at this moment, it would not perform the B=3 and would therefore continue onto whatever is the next statement. At this juncture, B would still have the value of 0.

For purposes of human readability of my code, I can include indentation and spaces to make the code hopefully easier to look at and understand. I don't have to use indentation and I don't have to use spaces for purposes of trying to make my code look "prettier" – the computer doesn't care per se and will ignore the indentation and the use of spaces for formatting purposes. It would be like writing a story and opting to use indentation and possibly lots of spaces between the sentences, which doesn't change the meaning of the story and it is just easier for other humans to potentially read the story.

The IF statement can be stated by using the upper case "IF" or it can be stated by the use of a lower case of "if"(or even mixed case) – you can decide which you think is easier for other humans to look at when the read your code.

The IF statement can be more elaborate in that you can also have multiple statements that you want to have performed when the condition is assessed to be true. To allow for multiple statements, you would use curly braces or brackets, putting a left curly brace to start the series of statements, which looks like this "{" and then a right curly brace to signify the end of the series of statements, which looks like this "}" and would then be followed by the semi-colon to end the entire IF statement.

That's enough for now about the IF statement.

A statement that says GO TO is indicated by using "GOTO" in caps or "goto" in lower case (or can be mixed case), and then provides a label to which the flow of the program will jump to during execution, and the statement has a semi-colon to signify the tail-end of the statement. This kind of statement allows you to alter the flow of the statements being performed.

The label must exist in the program and it is designated by using the label somewhere in the program and having a colon that follows the label where it has been placed in the code.

Here's a quick code example:

```
A = 1;
B = 0;
GOTO aardvark;
B = 8;
aardvark: C = 1;
```

This sets A to 1, B to 0. Then, the GO TO statement indicates that the code should find the statement labeled with the label of "aardvark" and proceed at that point in the code. In doing so, the code would then set the variable C to 1.

As a question for you, what would be the value of B at the time that the variable C is being set to the value of 1?

You should realize that B would 0. It would not be 8. The statement that says B=8 is after the GO TO statement and won't be reached, since instead the code is going to jump past it and proceed with the labeled statement of "aardvark" and won't therefore execute the B=8 statement.

In inspecting this code, there doesn't seem to be any means by which the line that says B=8 is going to be performed. It sits in a no man's land. The GO TO that precedes it will jump past it.

This kind of code that is unreachable is often referred to as dead code. It is dead code because it will never be brought to life, in the sense that it will never be executed during the course of the program being run.

Why would you have any dead code in your program? Normally, you would not. A programmer ought to be making sure that their is code is reachable in one manner or another. Having code that is unreachable is essentially unwise since it is sitting in the program but won't ever do anything. Furthermore, it can be quite confusing to any other programmer that comes along to take a look at the code.

There are times at which a programmer might purposely put dead code into their program and have in mind that at some future time they will come back to the code and change things so that the dead code then becomes reachable. In that sense, they are putting the dead code into the program as a kind of placeholder and have the intent to come around to it at some later time of doing further programming.

Another possibility is that the code was earlier being used, and for some reason the programmer decided they no longer wanted it to be executed, so they purposely put it into a spot that it became dead code in the program, or routed the execution around the code so that it would no longer be reachable and thus be dead code. They might for the moment want to keep the code inside the program, just in case they later decide to encompass it again to be executable, or maybe they want the code kept in the program so that some other programmer that wrote the now dead code can see what has become of their formerly executable code.

You can also make an argument that having dead code is a waste of the effort by the compiler that is generating the executable program. It is somewhat senseless to have the compiler go the trouble to syntactically analyze the dead code and produce something that won't be executed anyway.

Generally, the dead code is more of a human programmer consideration in that if a programmer has purposely included dead code it raises questions about why and what it is there for, since it won't be executed.

There is a strong possibility that the programmer goofed-up and didn't intend to have dead code.

Our inspection of the code won't immediately tell us whether the programmer put the dead code there for a purposeful reason, or they might have accidentally formulated a circumstance of dead code and not even realize they did so.

That's going to be bad because the programmer presumably assumed that the dead code would get executed at some juncture while the program was running, but it won't.

You are now ready to see the infamous code.

I'll start by showing just an excerpt, allowing you to focus on the specific matter at-hand.

After doing so, I'll then show you a large clip of the code to let you see a larger context of it. By the way, this source code is readily available as open source and can be found at numerous online sites.

Here it is:

```
if ((err = ReadyHash(&SSLHashSHA1, &hashCtx)) != 0)
    goto fail;
if ((err = SSLHashSHA1.update(&hashCtx, &clientRandom)) != 0)
    goto fail;
if ((err = SSLHashSHA1.update(&hashCtx, &serverRandom)) != 0)
    goto fail;
if ((err = SSLHashSHA1.update(&hashCtx, &signedParams)) != 0)
    goto fail;
    goto fail;
if ((err = SSLHashSHA1.final(&hashCtx, &hashOut)) != 0)
    goto fail;

err = sslRawVerify(ctx,
            ctx->peerPubKey,
            dataToSign,          /* plaintext */
            dataToSignLen,       /* plaintext length */
            signature,
            signatureLen);

if(err) {
    sslErrorLog("SSLDecodeSignedServerKeyExchange: sslRawVerify "
        "returned %d\n", (int)err);
    goto fail;
}

fail:
    SSLFreeBuffer(&signedHashes);
    SSLFreeBuffer(&hashCtx);
    return err;
```

The code might look daunting, but let's take a moment to walk through it and you'll see that it is able to be understood by simply knowing about IF statements and GO TO statements.

There is an IF statement at the beginning of the excerpt, which has a rather ugly looking condition, but you don't need to care what the condition says. Instead, merely notice that it has a condition, which is bounded by the left and right parentheses, and asks whether the ugly looking portion is not equal to 0.

We've already covered the aspect that if the condition turns out to be true, the next thing performed is the statement that is included within the scope of the IF statement, in this case, it is a GO TO that says "goto fail" and ends the IF statement.

Without being worried about the significance of the condition that is contained in the IF statement, just say to yourself that if the condition turns out to be true, the program will jump to the labeled area that has the label of "fail" (which is toward the end of the program excerpt that I've shown).

Observe that there appear to be five such IF statements, one after another.

Each of the IF statements seems to be somewhat the same, namely each tests a condition and if the condition is true then the code is going to jump to the label of "fail" that is further down in the code.

All of this would otherwise not be especially worth discussing, except for the fact that there is a "goto fail" hidden amongst that set of a series of five IF statements.

It is actually on its own and not part of any of those IF statements.

It is sitting in there, among those IF statements, and will be executed unconditionally, meaning that once it is reached, the program will do as instructed and jump to the label "fail" that appears further down in the code.

Can you see the extra "goto fail" that has found its ways into that series of IF statements?

It might take a bit of an eagle eye for you to spot it. In case you don't readily see it, I'll include the excerpt again here and show you just the few statements I want you to focus on for now:

```
if ((err = SSLHashSHA1.update(&hashCtx, &signedParams)) != 0)
    goto fail;
    goto fail;
if ((err = SSLHashSHA1.final(&hashCtx, &hashOut)) != 0)
    goto fail;
```

What you have in a more abstract way is these three statements:

```
IF (condition) goto fail;
goto fail;
IF (condition) go to fail;
```

There is an IF statement, the first of those above three lines, that has its own indication of jumping to the label "fail" when the assessed condition is true.

Immediately after that IF statement, there is a statement that says "goto fail" and it is all on its own, that's the second line of the three lines.

The IF statement that follows that "goto fail" which is on its own, the third line, won't ever be executed.

Why? Because the "goto fail" in front of it will branch away and the sad and lonely IF statement won't get executed.

In fact, all of the lines of code following that "goto fail" are going to be skipped during execution. They are in essence unreachable code.

They are dead code.

When you looked at those three statements in the original code, it had the unconditional "goto fail" indented over, like this (I'll bold it herein to make it standout for you):

```
IF (condition)
    goto fail;
    goto fail;
IF (condition)
    go to fail;
```

By the indentation, it becomes somewhat harder to discern that the unconditional GO TO statement exists within the sequence of those IF statements.

We found a part of this program that contains dead code. It has the dead code because there is this GO TO statement that is somewhat hidden amongst a small forest of IF statements. The indentation helps make the unconditional GO TO statement seem less obvious to the eye.

One line of code, a seemingly extraneous GO TO statement, which is placed in a manner that it creates a chunk of unreachable code. This is the weakest link in this chain. And it creates a lot of troubles.

Now that you've hopefully seen the manifestation of the GO TO statement, known widely as "goto fail" because that's what it says, I'll tell you why the unconditional GO TO statement created a ruckus.

By the way, most people tend to refer to this as the "goto fail goto fail" because it has two such statements together. There were T-shirts, bumper stickers, coffee mugs, and the like, all quickly put into the marketplace at the time of this incident, allowing the populace to relish the matter and showcase what it was about. Some of the versions said "goto fail; goto fail;" and included the proper semi-colons while others omitted the semi-colons.

What was the overall purpose of this program, you might be wondering?

It was an essential part of the software that does security verification for various Apple devices like their smartphones, iPad, etc.

You might be aware that when you try to access a web site, there is a kind of handshake that allows a secure connection to be potentially established. The standard used for this is referred to as the SSL/TSL, or the Secure Socket Layer / Transport Security Layer.

When your device tries to connect with a web site and SSL/TSL is being used, the device starts to make the connection, the web site presents a cryptographic certificate for verification purposes, and your device then tries to verify that the certificate is genuine (along with other validations that occur).

In the excerpt that I've shown you, you are looking at the software that would be sitting in your Apple device and trying to undertake that SSL/TSL verification.

The first part of the excerpt has to do with calculating a cryptographic checksum (hadn't shown that to you yet, didn't want to overwhelm, but I've shown a larger more contextual excerpt at the end of this narrative), and then doing a series of IF statements to see whether its any good or not.

You've already been looking closely via my walk-through at the IF statements and with your eagle eye you spotted that there is an extra GO TO statement of an unconditional nature which jumps over code that is therefore unreachable and considered dead code.

Unfortunately, regrettably, the dead code is quite important to the act of validating the SSL/TSL certificate and other factors.

Essentially, by bypassing an important part of the code, this program is going to be falsely reporting that the certificate is OK, under circumstances when it is not.

You might find of interest this official vendor declaration about the code when it was initially realized what was happening, and a quick fix was put in place: "Secure Transport failed to validate the authenticity of the connection. This issue was addressed by restoring missing validation steps."

You might quibble with the wording that says the validation steps were missing. They were there and yet were being skipped by the errant GO TO statement. I suppose though the fact that it says those missing validation steps were restored is somewhat the case, namely that if you were to remove the offending GO TO statement it would allow the "missing" (more like skipped) steps to be "restored" (become reachable and therefore executed).

In what way could this problem have been exploited (prior to being fixed)?

Basically, you could potentially trick a device that was connecting to a web site and place yourself into the middle, doing so to surreptitiously watch and read the traffic going back-and-forth, grabbing up private info which you might use for nefarious purposes. This is commonly known as the Man-in-the-Middle security attack (MITM). It would be relatively easy to undertake that exploit if you knew that the software was skipping doing the proper set of verification checks.

I've now provided you with an example of a hole in the dam. It is a seemingly small hole, yet it undermined a much larger dam. Among a length chain of things that need to occur for the security aspects of the SSL/TSL, this one weak link undermined a lot of it. I do want to make sure that you know that it was not completely undermined since some parts of the code were working as intended and it was this particular slice that had the issue.

There are an estimated 2,000 lines of code in this one program. Out of the 2,000 lines of code, one line, the infamous extra "goto fail" had caused the overall program to now falter in terms of what it was intended to achieve.

That means that only 0.05% of the code was "wrong" and yet it undermined the entire program.

You can argue whether it is fair or not to count the line of code against the two thousand lines, and we might use some other metric, maybe making this seem not so bad. But you could also say that the 2,000 is an "undercount" number and we ought to include the many other thousands of lines of code found in the allied programs that relate to the purpose of this program.

Some would describe this as an exemplar of being brittle.

Presumably, we don't want most things in our lives to be brittle. We want them to be robust. We want them to be resilient. The placement of just one line of code in the wrong spot and then undermining a significant overall intent is seemingly not something we would agree to be properly robust or resilient.

Fortunately, this instance did not seem to cause any known security breaches to get undertaken and no lives were lost. Imagine though that this were to happen inside a real-time system that is controlling a robotic arm in a manufacturing plant. Suppose the code worked most of the time, but on a rare occasion it reached a spot of this same kind of unconditional GO TO, and perhaps jumped past code that checks to make sure that a human is not in the way of the moving robotic arm. By bypassing that verification code, the consequences could be dire.

For the story of the Dutch boy that plugged the hole in the dam, we are never told how the hole got there in the first place. It is a mystery, though most people that read the story just take it at face value that there was a hole. The focus became what to do about the hole, rather than trying to figure out how the hole arose. This makes sense to proceed to fix the problem, doing so as quickly as possible, and perhaps allowing the "how" or "why" to sit undiscovered.

I'd like to take a moment and speculate about the infamous GO TO of the "goto fail" and see if we can learn any additional lessons by doing so.

At the time that it was discovered, the typical refrain from many was "how the heck did that extra goto fail get in there?" I've cleaned-up the language used, as it usually consisted of flavorful four-letter words, harsher than the word heck.

Nobody seems to know how it actually happened, well, I'm sure someone does that was involved in the code, but by-and-large it seems that nobody overall seems to know or has definitively come out publicly to say. We are left to speculate.

Let's start with the theories that I think are most entertaining but seem farfetched, in my opinion.

One theory is that it was purposely planted into the code, doing so at the request of someone such as perhaps the NSA. This would presumably allow for the NSA or whomever that made the request to be able to secretly have a hole that they could use at their discretion.

It's a nifty theory because you can couple with it that the use of the single GO TO statement makes the matter seem as though it was an innocent mistake. What better way to plant a backdoor and yet if it is later discovered you can say that it was merely an accident all along. Sweet! If the code was written in a more conniving way, we might be immediately suspicious once the code came to light. This use of the one GO TO statement is the seemingly ideal means to defuse any concern once it becomes discovered.

Of course, the conspiracy theorists say that's what they want us to think, namely that it was just a pure accident. Hogwash, they say, it was the clever hand of someone that knew what they were doing. Perhaps it involved lengthy discussions of how-to best plant it so that later on it would not seem like a plant. Maybe they went back-and-forth on a dozen ways to do it and landed on this beauty.

Sorry, I'm not buying into the conspiracy theory on this. Yes, I realize it means that maybe I've been bamboozled. And, maybe I'm now helping those conspirators to keep you in the dark too. Ugh!

Another theory is that the programmer or programmers (we don't know for sure if it was one programmer, and so maybe it was several that got together on this), opted to plant the GO TO statement and keep it in their back pocket. This is the kind of thing you might try to sell on the dark web. There are a slew of zero-day exploits that untoward hackers trade and sell, so why not do the same with this?

Once again, this seems to almost make sense because the beauty is that the hole is based on just one GO TO statement. This might provide plausible deniability if the code is tracked to whomever put the GO TO statement in there. What, me, the programmer or programmers might say, I guess I somehow accidentally got that mixed into the code. Meanwhile, their Swiss bank account or their bitcoin account has a sizable deposit in it.

I'm going to vote against this purposeful hacking theory. I realize that I might be falling for someone's scam and they are laughing all the way to the bank about it. I don't think so. Part of my logic is that it really doesn't seem like the kind of thing you would do if you were really trying to have a hidden treasure. The same logic applies to my knocking down the conspiracy theory.

In any case, now let's dispense with those theories and got toward something that I think has a much higher chance of approaching what really did happen.

First, we'll divide the remaining options into something that was mistakenly done versus something intentionally done.

I'll cover the "mistakenly done" theories first.

You are a harried programmer. You are churning out gobs of code. You've been assigned this SSL/TSL code. Let's assume you write this thing from scratch. You come up with a series of conditionals that you want to do as part of the verification portion of the code.

While writing those IF statements, you accidentally fat finger an extra "goto fail" into the code. At the time, you've indented it and so it appears to be in the right spot. When you are looking at your code, doing so several times, each time your eye glides down the screen of where you are developing your code and you see those several IF statements. They all look good. You've checked and rechecked the conditions themselves to make sure they are the right aspects to be checked.

By mistake, you have placed that line into your code. Because it is indented and because the line above it is the same, stating "goto fail" as well, and because you know in your mind that the IF statements are all supposed to jump to the "fail" label when they catch an error, you don't notice that extra GO TO statement. It becomes part of the landscape of the code.

That's one theory about the mistakenly angle.

Another theory is that the programmer had intended to put another IF statement into that segment of the code and had typed the "goto fail" portion, but then somehow got distracted or interrupted and neglected to put the first part, the IF statement part itself, into the code.

Yet another variation is that there was an IF statement there, but the programmer for some reason opted to delete it, but when the programmer did the delete, they mistakenly did not remove the "goto fail" which would have been easy to miss because it was on the next physical line.

We can also play with the idea that there might have been multiple programmers involved.

Suppose one programmer wrote part of that portion with the IF statements, and another programmer was also working on the code, using another instance, and when the two instances got merged together, the merging led to the extra GO TO statement.

This could have happened by the automation tool used to do the merge, or might have been done by the programmer(s) opting to do the merge manually or they were trying to do some clean-up after the merge.

On a similar front, there is a bunch of IF statements earlier in the code. Maybe those IF statements were copied and used for this set of IF statements, and when the programmer or programmers were cleaning up the copied IF statements, they inadvertently added the unconditional GO TO statement.

Let's shift our attention to the "intentional" theories of how the line got in there. I'm going to put aside any versions of the intentional theory that have to do with wanting to be nefarious, which I've already earlier covered. Instead, I'll focus on intentions that were innocent and regretfully went awry.

The programmer was writing the code and after having written those series of IF statements, took another look and thought they had forgotten to put a "goto fail" for the IF statement that precedes the now known to be wrong GO TO statement. In their mind, they thought they were putting in the line because it needed to go there.

Or, maybe the programmer had been doing some testing of the code. While doing testing, the programmer opted to temporarily put the GO TO into the series of IF statements, wanting to momentarily short circuit the rest of the routine. This was handy at the time. Unfortunately, the programmer forgot to remove it later on.

Or, another programmer was inspecting the code. Being rushed or distracted, the programmer thought that a GO TO opt to be in the mix of those IF statements. We know now that this isn't a logical thing to do, but perhaps at the time, in the mind of the programmer, it was conceived that the GO TO was going to have some other positive effect, and so they put it into the code.

Programmers are human beings. They make mistakes. They can have one thing in mind about the code, and yet the code might actually end-up doing something other than what they thought.

Some people were quick to judge that the programmer must have been a rookie to have let this happen. I'm not so sure that we can say that the programmer was naïve or junior or whatever, due to this particular instance.

I've known and managed many programmers and software engineers that were topnotch, seasoned with many years of complex systems projects, and yet they too made mistakes, doing so and yet at first insistent to the extreme that they must be right, having recalcitrant chagrin afterward when proven to be wrong.

This then takes us to another perspective, namely if any of those aforementioned theories about the mistaken action or the intentional action are true, how come it wasn't caught?

Typically, many software teams do code reviews. This might involve merely having another developer eyeball your code, or it might be more exhaustive and involve you walking them through it, including each trying to prove or disprove that the code is proper and complete.

Would this error have been caught by a code review? Maybe yes, maybe not.

This is somewhat insidious because it is only one line, and it was indented to fall into line with the other lines, helping to mask it or at least camouflage it by appearing to be nicely woven into the code. I'm not saying that's a basis for not having caught it during code review, and only explaining how it could have survived a code review.

Suppose the code review was surface level and involved simply eyeballing the code. That kind of code review could easily miss catching this GO TO statement issue.

Suppose it was noticed during code review, but it was put to the side for a future look-see, and then because the programmers were doing a thousand things at once, oops it got left in the code. That's another real possibility. Not pretty, but realistic.

You also need to consider the human aspects of trust and belief in the skills of the other programmers involved in a programming team.

Suppose the programmer that wrote this code was considered topnotch. Time after time, their code was flawless. On this particular occasion, when it came to doing a code review, it was a slimmer code review because of the trust placed in that programmer. Unfortunately, this was the rare instance in which they messed-up.

When managing software engineers, they sometimes will get huffy at me when I have them do code reviews. There are some that will say they are professionals and don't need a code review, or that if there is a code review it should be quick and lite because of how good they are. I respect their skill sets but try to point out that any of us can have something mar our work.

One aspect that is very hard to get across involves the notion of egoless coding and code reviews. The notion is that you try to separate the person from the code in terms of the aspect that any kind of critiquing of the code becomes an attack on that person. This means that no one wants to do these code reviews when it spirals downward into a hatred fest. What can happen is the code reviews become an unseemly quagmire of accusations and anger, spilling out based not only on the code but perhaps due to other personal animosity too.

Besides code reviews, one could say that this GO TO statement should have been found during testing of the code.

Certainly, it would seem at the unit level of testing, you could have setup a test suite of cases that fed into this routine, and you would have discovered that sometimes the verification was passing when it should not be.

This would have gotten someone to take another look into the code and they most likely would have eventually found the extra GO TO statement (doing so by asking the question of how were those other lines of code not being executed).

Perhaps the unit testing was done in a shallow way. By luck, or unluck, they did not have a sufficient range and depth of prepared test cases that encountered this issue. Most developers tend to dislike having to do testing. They will often do their own ad hoc testing and when it comes to doing more complete testing, will give it short shrift.

If you separate the duties of formal testing by someone else from the person that wrote the code, it can sometimes overcome this inherent reluctance to fully test the code. The original programmer might feel that there is no reason to test certain kinds of cases, since "they know" it works for those. Meanwhile, someone else that is earnestly doing testing, might not have such a bias. I'm not saying it always works that way, and it can be that the tester is unfamiliar with the code and therefore does not necessarily do a better job of testing it.

We might also wonder what happened at doing a system test.

Normally, you put together the various units or multiple pieces and do a test across the whole system or subsystem. If they did so, how did this get missed? Again, it could be that the test cases used at the system level did not encompass anything that ultimately rolled down into this particular routine and would have showcased the erroneous result. This might be a poorly chosen set of system test cases, or they might have been under-the-gun to get things completed and weren't able or had the resources to do more exhaustive overall testing.

You might wonder how the compiler itself missed this aspect. Some compilers can do a kind of static analysis trying to find things that might be awry, such as dead code. Apparently, at the time, there was speculation that the compiler could have helped, but it had options that were either confusing to use, or when used were often mistaken in what they found.

I'm sure that any programmer that dealt with such a mess would probably believe that the chances of the compiler helping versus causing them more anguish made them decide to forego using such options.

We can take a different perspective and question how the code itself is written and structured overall.

One aspect that is often done but should be typically reconsidered is that the "err" value that gets used in this routine and sent back to the rest of the software was set initially to being Okay, and only once something found an untoward does it get set to a Not Okay signal. This meant that when the verification code was skipped, the flag was defaulting to everything being Okay.

One might argue that this is the opposite of the right way to do things. Maybe you ought to assume that the verification is Not Okay, and the routine has to essentially go through all the verifications to set the value to Okay. In this manner, if somehow the routine short circuits early, at least the verification is stated as Not Okay. This would seem like a safer default in such a case.

Another aspect would be the use of curly braces or brackets. Remember that I had earlier stated you can use those on an IF statement. Besides having use for multiple statements on an IF, it also can be a visual indicator for a human programmer of the start and end of the body of statements. Some believe that if the programmer had used the curly braces, the odds are that the extra "goto fail" would have stuck out more so as a sore thumb. I'm not so sure that's really what would have happened, though it might have helped.

We can also question the use of the multiple IF's in a series. This is often done by programmers, and it is a kind of easy (some say sloppy or lazy) way to do things, but there are other programming techniques and constructs that can be used instead. I say this because the series of IF statements can be a mind numbing and visually numbing portrayal and allow this kind of inadvertent issue to occur.

There are some that have attacked the use of the GO TO statements throughout the code passage. You might be aware that there has been an ongoing debate about the "dangers" of using GO TO statements. Some have said it is a construct that should be banned entirely. Perhaps the debate was most vividly started when Edgar Dijkstra had his letter published in the *Communications of the ACM* in March of 1968. The debate about the merits versus the downsides of the GO TO have continued since then.

You could restructure this code to eliminate the GO TO statements, in which case, the extra GO TO would never have gotten into the mix, presumably.

Another aspect involves the notion that the "goto fail" is repeated in the offending portion, which some would say should have actually made it visually standout. So far, I've suggested that it was somewhat hidden from view, due to the other nearby lines of code and the use of indentation. Would your eye tend to catch the same line of code repeated twice like this, especially a somewhat naked GO TO statement? Apparently, presumably, it did not. Some say the compiler should have issued a warning about a seemingly repeated line, even if it wasn't set to detect dead code.

You might also point out that this code doesn't seem to have much built-in self-checking going on. You can write your code to "just get the job done" and it then provides its result. Another approach involves adding additional layers of code that do various double-checks. If that had been built into this code, maybe it would have detected that the verification was not being done to a full extent, and whatever error handling should take place would then have gotten invoked.

In the software field, we often speak of the smell of a piece of code. Code-smell means that the code might be poorly written or suspect in one manner or another, and upon taking a sniff or a whiff of it (by looking at the code), one might detect a foul odor, possibly even a stench.

I know that most developers use the metaphor in that manner, while I at times try to make it not just about the negative, but also about the positive.

I at times remark that someone's code has a refreshing odor, a pleasant and pleasing odor to it. That's code that is well devised, well written, and has the right kinds of built-in error checking to go along with it.

Software developers also refer to technical debt. This means that when you right somewhat foul code, your creating a kind of debt that will someday be due. It's like taking out a loan, and eventually the loan will need to be paid back. Bad code will almost always boomerang and eventually come back to haunt. I try to impart among my software developers that we ought to be creating technical credit, meaning that we've structured and written the code for future ease of maintenance and growth. We have planted the seed for this, even if at the time that we developed the code we didn't necessarily need to do so.

As a long-time programmer and software engineer, I am admittedly sympathetic to the plight of fellow software developers. It is always easy to do second guessing. There is inevitably that hindsight that seems to be 20-20.

For those that want to dump the matter onto the shoulders of the programmer that did this particular work of the "goto fail" issue, we can do so, but I think we need to have a context associated with it.

Suppose the programmer was hampered and not being provided by sufficient tools to do their work. Suppose the manager was pushing the programmer to just get the work done. Suppose the schedule was unrealistic and shortcuts were taken. It takes a village to develop software. If the village is not of the right culture and approach, you are going to get software that matches to that culture.

I am not letting individual developers off-the-hook. I am saying though that it is hard to go against the grain of your manager, your team, your company culture, if it isn't allowing you to do the kind of robust and resilient programming that you think ought to be done. It is hard to be the one that is trying to turn the tide.

At the same time, I also want to point out that sometimes there are developers that aren't versed in how to make their software robust or resilient. They have done software development and it seems to work out okay for them. They might not know of other ways to get the job done. Does the company try to ensure that the developers are aware of various techniques and approaches? Does the company reward such work? If not, it's going to be a street fight style of coding. As some say, there is no style in a street fight, and you do whatever you can to survive.

What does this have to do with AI self-driving cars?

At the Cybernetic AI Self-Driving Car Institute, we are developing AI software for self-driving cars. The auto makers and tech firms doing likewise are hopefully doing the right thing in terms of how they are developing their software, meaning that they need to recognize the dangers of the brittleness of the AI systems they are crafting.

Brittleness of the AI for an AI self-driving car is quite serious. If the AI encounters a weak link, imagine if it happens when the self-driving car is doing 65 miles per hour on a crowded freeway. Lives are at stake. This AI is a real-time system involving multi-ton cars that can quickly and in a deadly manner determine the life or death of humans.

Allow me to further elaborate.

I'd like to first clarify and introduce the notion that there are varying levels of AI self-driving cars. The topmost level is considered Level 5. A Level 5 self-driving car is one that is being driven by the AI and there is no human driver involved. For the design of Level 5 self-driving cars, the auto makers are even removing the gas pedal, brake pedal, and steering wheel, since those are contraptions used by human drivers. The Level 5 self-driving car is not being driven by a human and nor is there an expectation that a human driver will be present in the self-driving car. It's all on the shoulders of the AI to drive the car.

For self-driving cars less than a Level 5, there must be a human driver present in the car. The human driver is currently considered the responsible party for the acts of the car. The AI and the human driver are co-sharing the driving task. In spite of this co-sharing, the human is supposed to remain fully immersed into the driving task and be ready at all times to perform the driving task. I've repeatedly warned about the dangers of this co-sharing arrangement and predicted it will produce many untoward results.

Let's focus herein on the true Level 5 self-driving car. Much of the comments apply to the less than Level 5 self-driving cars too, but the fully autonomous AI self-driving car will receive the most attention in this discussion.

Here's the usual steps involved in the AI driving task:

- Sensor data collection and interpretation
- Sensor fusion
- Virtual world model updating
- AI action planning
- Car controls command issuance

Another key aspect of AI self-driving cars is that they will be driving on our roadways in the midst of human driven cars too. There are some pundits of AI self-driving cars that continually refer to a utopian world in which there are only AI self-driving cars on the public roads. Currently there are about 250+ million conventional cars in the United States alone, and those cars are not going to magically disappear or become true Level 5 AI self-driving cars overnight.

Indeed, the use of human driven cars will last for many years, likely many decades, and the advent of AI self-driving cars will occur while there are still human driven cars on the roads. This is a crucial point since this means that the AI of self-driving cars needs to be able to contend with not just other AI self-driving cars, but also contend with human driven cars. It is easy to envision a simplistic and rather unrealistic world in which all AI self-driving cars are politely interacting with each other and being civil about roadway interactions. That's not what is going to be happening for the foreseeable future. AI self-driving cars and human driven cars will need to be able to cope with each other.

Returning to the topic of the "goto fail" and AI brittleness, we all need to realize that such a one line of code could upset the AI self-driving car cart, so to speak.

In theory, the AI systems of AI self-driving cars should have numerous checks-and-balances. The chances of any single line of code causing havoc should be extremely low. There should be fail-safe capabilities. The testing should be extremely extensive and exhaustive. Simulations should be used to help ferret out such anomalies prior to getting into the code of a roadway running self-driving car. And so on.

That's the theory of it.

The real-world is different. In many of these AI systems there are tons of third-party code that is being used, and other packages and open source being used. For the AI developers tasked with developing the AI of the self-driving cars, they are likely assuming that those other bodies of code are already well-tested and will work as intended.

Maybe yes, maybe no.

There is such tremendous pressure to get AI self-driving cars onto the streets, pushed by this relentless idea that whomever is first will somehow win this moonshot race, there is likely a substantial amount of cutting of corners in terms of code reviews, tools being used, and the like.

Many of the AI developers came from university settings, wherein they mainly did prototypes or proof of concept versions of their AI systems. They might not be familiar with the real-time demands of a production system that has to work in public roadways in a highly reliable and safe manner. Their capabilities as software engineers are likely to be somewhat limited. They might be well-versed in AI, but not how to scale-up software that has to work in a highly complex environment.

I realize that some will say that this is yet another reason to rely upon Machine Learning and Deep Learning. Rather than writing code, you presumably can base your AI system for a self-driving car on the use of packages that can emit a large-scale artificial neural network and let that be the core of your AI for the driving task.

At this time, the AI stack for self-driving cars is still primarily of a more traditional nature and the Machine Learning and Deep Learning is mainly for only selected elements, most notably for the sensor data analyses. The rest of the AI is done the old-fashioned way, and for which the single line of code and weak link are a real possibility.

I don't want to leave you with the impression that somehow the Machine Learning and Deep Learning is a silver bullet in this matter. It is not.

The packages used for the Machine Learning and Deep Learning could certainly have their own weaknesses in them. The resultant runnable neural network might be flawed due to some flaw within the Machine Learning or Deep Learning code itself. The executable might be flawed. We already know that the neural network itself can be "flawed" in that you can do various sensory trickery to fool some of the large-scale neural networks being constructed.

We've already seen some incidents of AI self-driving cars that highlight the points I've been making about the importance of resiliency and robustness.

Sadly, as I've been warning in my writings and presentations, we are going to see more blood spilled by AI self-driving cars and it won't be a simple waving of the hands anymore that somehow the humans in the car were at fault. It's going to be that the AI system was at fault.

Conclusion

The Dutch boy stopped the dam from breaking by plugging the hole with his finger. Heroic! We can all rejoice in the tale. It provides us with the realization that sometimes small things can have a big impact. There is the lesson that the weakest link, this seemingly inconsequential hole, could lead to much greater ruin.

How many of today's budding AI self-driving cars are right now underway and have a hole somewhere deep inside them, waiting to become the spigot that regrettably causes the rest of the AI system to go awry and a terrible result occurs. Nobody knows.

How much effort are the auto makers and tech firms putting toward finding the hole or holes beforehand?

How many are putting in place error handling and error processing that once a hole arises during actual use and after deployment, the AI will be able to recognize and deal safely with the hole?

I hope that the tale of the Dutch boy will spark attention to this matter.

I tried to showcase how this can happen in the real-world by making use of the infamous "goto fail goto fail" incident.

It is a nice choice for this purpose since it is easily understood and readily publicly discussed. No need to search high and far to find some seemingly arcane example that most would try to write-off as inconsequential.

There is a huge body of water sitting at the dam, which we'll say is the public and their already nervous qualms about AI self-driving cars. If even one hole opens up in that dam, I assure you the water is going to gush through it, and we'll likely see a tsunami of regulation and backlash against the advent of AI self-driving cars.

I don't want that.

I hope the rest of you don't want that.

Let's make sure to put in place the appropriate efforts to seek out the weakest links in our AI systems and find them before it finds your AI self-driving car system, so we can keep it from destroying the whole dam.

OPEN SOURCE CODE OF GOTO FAIL BUG

```
static OSStatus
SSLVerifySignedServerKeyExchange(SSLContext *ctx, bool
isRsa, SSLBuffer signedParams,
                    uint8_t *signature, UInt16 signatureLen)
{
    OSStatus      err;
    SSLBuffer     hashOut, hashCtx, clientRandom, serverRandom;
    uint8_t       hashes[SSL_SHA1_DIGEST_LEN + SSL_MD5_DIGEST_LEN];
    SSLBuffer     signedHashes;
    uint8_t       *dataToSign;
    size_t        dataToSignLen;
```

```
signedHashes.data = 0;
hashCtx.data = 0;

clientRandom.data = ctx->clientRandom;
clientRandom.length = SSL_CLIENT_SRVR_RAND_SIZE;
serverRandom.data = ctx->serverRandom;
serverRandom.length = SSL_CLIENT_SRVR_RAND_SIZE;


if(isRsa) {
    /* skip this if signing with DSA */
    dataToSign = hashes;
    dataToSignLen = SSL_SHA1_DIGEST_LEN + SSL_MD5_DIGEST_LEN;
    hashOut.data = hashes;
    hashOut.length = SSL_MD5_DIGEST_LEN;

    if ((err = ReadyHash(&SSLHashMD5, &hashCtx)) != 0)
        goto fail;
    if ((err = SSLHashMD5.update(&hashCtx, &clientRandom)) != 0)
        goto fail;
    if ((err = SSLHashMD5.update(&hashCtx, &serverRandom)) != 0)
        goto fail;
    if ((err = SSLHashMD5.update(&hashCtx, &signedParams)) != 0)
        goto fail;
     if ((err = SSLHashMD5.final(&hashCtx, &hashOut)) != 0)
        goto fail;
}
else {
    /* DSA, ECDSA - just use the SHA1 hash */
    dataToSign = &hashes[SSL_MD5_DIGEST_LEN];
    dataToSignLen = SSL_SHA1_DIGEST_LEN;
}
```

```
hashOut.data = hashes + SSL_MD5_DIGEST_LEN;
hashOut.length = SSL_SHA1_DIGEST_LEN;
if ((err = SSLFreeBuffer(&hashCtx)) != 0)
   goto fail;

if ((err = ReadyHash(&SSLHashSHA1, &hashCtx)) != 0)
   goto fail;
if ((err = SSLHashSHA1.update(&hashCtx, &clientRandom)) != 0)
   goto fail;
if ((err = SSLHashSHA1.update(&hashCtx, &serverRandom)) != 0)
   goto fail;
if ((err = SSLHashSHA1.update(&hashCtx, &signedParams)) != 0)
   goto fail;
   goto fail;
if ((err = SSLHashSHA1.final(&hashCtx, &hashOut)) != 0)
   goto fail;

err = sslRawVerify(ctx,
               ctx->peerPubKey,
               dataToSign,          /* plaintext */
               dataToSignLen,       /* plaintext length */
               signature,
               signatureLen);
if(err) {
   sslErrorLog("SSLDecodeSignedServerKeyExchange: sslRawVerify "
         "returned %d\n", (int)err);
   goto fail;
}

fail:
   SSLFreeBuffer(&signedHashes);
   SSLFreeBuffer(&hashCtx);
   return err;
```

CHAPTER 5

SCRABBLE UNDERSTANDING AND AI SELF-DRIVING CARS

CHAPTER 5

SCRABBLE

UNDERSTANDING

AND

AI SELF-DRIVING CARS

The headlines blared that the winner of the French Scrabble World Championship was someone that did not understand a word of French. Sacrebleu!

Note that I spelled this stereotypical French phrase as it is spelled in the French language, as one word, rather than the Americanized version of two words with the accent (sacre bleu), which would be important if I was playing Scrabble right now. Essentially, it is an outdated and hackneyed curse that was never particularly used by the French but crept into the English language and employed for formulaic portrayals in movies and TV shows.

In any case, let's focus on the aspect that the winner of the World Champion for the Francophone Classic Scrabble in 2015 was a non-French speaking contestant. This feat seemed to be nearly impossible.

How could anyone manage to win in Scrabble, a board game dependent upon words, and yet not understand the words being used in this famous and popular sport? Bizarre, some said. A miracle, others stated.

I'd say it is nothing more than a magician pulling a rabbit out of a hat or finding your chosen card out of a deck of cards.

Let's unpack what it means to play Scrabble and see how this winner was able to succeed.

In Scrabble, there is a board consisting of squares arranged in a 15 by 15 grid. Players have various tiles of letters and are supposed to lay down the tiles in a manner that spells out a word. This can only be done by putting the tiles in a left-to-right or downward manner, meaning you cannot place words in a diagonal or written backwards. There are points scored per each tile placed onto the board. The board itself also has squares that when used will amplify the points scored.

What makes the game particularly challenging is that there is a limited set of letters, plus you need to build your word off of a word played on the board (other than at the start), there is a bag of the letters from which you draw your subset of letters, and a slew of other complicating factors come to play. The play of the game alternates between each of the players.

During your turn, you can playout some or all your tiles if there is a word that you can make, or you can pass but this means that you are giving up that turn and won't get any points, or you can do an exchange of your subset of letters with whatever remains in the bag and as randomly selected out of the bag.

When I used to play Scrabble with my children, they at first were eager to make a word whenever they could see that it was possible based on their tiles in-hand and what was available on the board. They quickly realized that the problem of impulsively wanting to make words is that you might be setting up your opponent to subsequently score points.

Soon enough, the kids soon realized that they needed to try and anticipate whether their opponent could make a word, and attempt to keep their opponent from doing so, by being mindful of the words they were making on the board.

I liked playing the Scrabble game with my kids because it led to discussions, sometimes debates, regarding whether a word was a real word or a made-up word. You see, playing Scrabble involves first deciding what definitive source will be used to dictate what is a word versus what is not a legitimate word. The kids might have had their own vocabulary from the playground of made-up words, like "sheez-la-cheese," but I explained that we'd instead use words that were only found in a valid dictionary.

So, we'd grab an English dictionary from our bookshelf and have it at the ready, using it to look up words and verify that they were valid. Even if I already knew a word that was considered in contention, I was happy and eager to see them looking up the word anyway. I figured this would be a means to boost their vocabulary.

Besides considering how the word was correctly spelled, I typically inquired as to the meaning of the word. I did so in hopes that the word would become enmeshed in their minds. If the word was merely a series of letters that happened to make a word, and yet if they did not know what the word meant, I figured it wouldn't do them much good. When it came time for them to take tests at school and write narratives, I wanted to ensure they knew the nature of the word and could use it in a sensible manner.

This last aspect about understanding the meaning of words is crucial to the story about the non-French speaking winner of the Francophone Scrabble Championship.

In Scrabble, there is no requirement that you actually understand the word that you are spelling out on the board. You don't have to state what the word means. The word merely has to be a valid word.

If you perchance have heard a word and know how it is spelled, or seen it written someplace, and yet if you have no clue what it means, you are perfectly Okay to use it during Scrabble. Nobody is going to ask you to explain the word or use it in a sentence, since that's not in the official rules of the game (though, when I played Scrabble with my kids, I added that as a rule, sneakily to get them to understand the words and expand their comprehension and vocabulary at the same time).

The non-French speaking contestant had done something that was impressive, he had memorized all of the words in the officially used French dictionary, doing so by only memorizing how the words were spelled. He happened to have a photographic memory capability and was able in nine weeks to memorize the words. He did not know what the French words meant.

He could not pronounce them per se, since he hadn't studied the verbalized versions of the words, though I'm sure he could have guessed at how to say many of the words. In that manner, it is perhaps a stretch to suggest that he was a non-French speaking person, due to the aspect that he had memorized French words and likely could try to utter them. He likely could also guess at many of the words in terms of their meanings, since French and English have many of the same underlying roots and bases.

In any case, it seems relatively fair to assert that he wasn't French speaking since he could not use the words in any fluent manner and had no understanding of the words, along with no grasp of how to form sentences and abide by the semantics of the language. He did though have to learn to count in French from one to ten, in order to participate in the Scrabble game, a requirement of the contestants.

I've now revealed how the magician pulled off the magic act. Similar to describing how a rabbit got into that hat of the magician, or how your card was marked or planted into a deck of cards, the secret in this case of Scrabble is that you don't need to understand the words and merely need to know how to spell them.

Admittedly, memorizing an entire dictionary of words is somewhat impressive, though having a photographic memory makes it relatively "easy" to do.

To him, the words were essentially icons or images. Sure, you ultimately need to discern each separate letter that is in a given word, but you can pretty much just remember what the word looks like and then have it ready when needed.

Pretend that letters are only scratches that consist of lines and curves. Those various lines and curves make letters, and the letters are placed next to each other to make words. It is a primitive way to consider the nature of words and letters, though quite effective and the only necessity for playing Scrabble. They are nothing more than blobs.

Upon hearing about this contestant winning, I was immediately aware that he would not have had to "understand" the French language to win at such a Scrabble tournament. Thus, I was not especially surprised or taken aback.

My first thought was that there is actually a lot more to Scrabble beyond memorizing patterns of letters and words. Being smart about the game play is essential, and especially at any vaunted tournament.

The strategies and tactics that you use in Scrabble are crucial to winning. You cannot just take anyone that happens to have a photographic memory and have them winning Scrabble contests all around the planet. It is like playing Poker, namely that being able to play by the rules and realize what the different cards in the deck represent won't let you win those million-dollar Las Vegas gambling contests. You need to have a ton of game-playing skills and hone them to be able to play at the top-level of competition.

It turns out that the winner of the Francophone Scrabble Championship was a five-time winner of the North American Scrabble Championships and a three-time winner of the World Scrabble Championships.

All of those competitions were in English. Regardless though of the language used in those competitions, the fact that he had won those contests demonstrated that he knew how to play the Scrabble game and must have finely tuned his strategies and tactics for it.

In that way, he was able to deploy his Scrabble playing expertise into the context of the French version, since it is still the same fundamental game. By memorizing the French words, he had put together a potent combination, consisting of his highly honed Scrabble game playing strategies and tactics, along with having at his fingertips (in his mind) an entire dictionary of allowed words. It was a kind of double-whammy that likely made things tough on his French-speaking competition.

One wonders how many of the other contestants had a photographic memory and had memorized as many words as he had? Probably not many of the contestants have that knack. Even if there were other contestants with a similarly sized word set in their minds, you then have the aspect of Scrabble game playing strategies and tactics. So, he might have bested some of them in that manner.

There is also the role of chance involved in the game, since you don't know beforehand what letters you will get. There is the randomness of drawing tiles (letters) from the bag. Presumably, if you play enough games, over time the "luck" or "unluck" of your draws will even out and the players will then be winning based on their actual game play expertise, though this is only likely if the number of games played is sufficiently large. Scrabble competitions try to deal with this matter by having multiple games between players, but in-the-small it is not necessarily the case that the luck factor is going to be expunged.

Another facet of the Scrabble game is the somewhat false assumption that by playing words with the largest number of letters that you'll be able to prevail in terms of getting the highest total score by the end of the game.

If you play a bunch of rounds, you'll learn soon enough that the largest words also tend to offer ripe opportunities for your competition. In fact, some studies have suggested that you are likely better off in using predominantly four-letter and five-letter words, assuming that you are playing strongly and that your opponent is also a strong player too.

Bringing up the topic of Scrabble will often elicit a smile from AI developers and they'll likely ask or point out gently that "didn't we solve that already" with AI? This makes me cringe somewhat because it is a bit of an overstatement.

Yes, there are some quite famous AI programs that do play Scrabble well. The most notable ones are Maven and Quackle.

Maven was first developed around the mid-1980s and became the star around which other offshoots tended to appear. The structure of Maven's approach consists of dividing a Scrabble match into a mid-game, a pre-endgame, and an endgame set of phases (the mid-game is somewhat a misnomer since it also serves as the start-game capability too).

During the mid-game portion, the AI of Maven is ascertaining all possible plays based on the tiles in the rack of the player and what's on the board and uses relatively simple rules or heuristics to try and figure out which of the valid words based on its rack might be most prudent to play. There is a simulation or "simming" done to try and look-ahead at various moves and counter-moves, though in the initial incarnations it was only a two-ahead look (a 2-ply deep). This is considered a truncated version of the Monte Carlo simulation and not a full-bodied MCTS (Monte Carlo Tree Search) implementation.

Other variants of Maven included the use of a DAWG (Directed Acyclic Word Graph), which tends to run fast and doesn't require an elaborate algorithm per se, and later used the GADDAG (this naming was intended to be smarmy, it is the letters DAG for Directed Acyclic, spelled backwards and then forwards).

The end-game is a different kind of challenge and kicks-in once the bag of letters is empty. This means that there is no longer a random draw of letters.

You might therefore assume that things are pretty simplified, since you then know all the letters already on the board, you know the letters in the racks, and so you presumably can handle a perfect information situation, which in the case of Maven the B-star search was utilized. Part of the difficulty is there is usually a time limit involved and the search space can become large and computationally expensive in terms of time consumed.

Quackle came along after Maven and employs many similar game playing approaches, along with a few other nuances. If you are interested in Scrabble AI game play, the Quackle is readily available as open source and can be found in places such as GitHub.

Both Maven and Quackle have had circumstances wherein they were used to compete against topnotch human Scrabble players.

Though they have had some impressive wins, it does not mean that they have "solved" the playing of Scrabble by AI. I emphasize this because of the sometimes smirks that I get from AI developers that believe there is nothing left to do in the Scrabble game regarding trying to use AI. Anyone that says this is either unaware of the reality of AI Scrabble game playing, or they assume that if there were some wins by AI Scrabble game playing system that it implies the matter is completed and no further effort would be worthwhile.

Somewhat similar to the non-French speaking human winner of the Francophone Scrabble Championship, there is an added edge in this particular kind of game if you can have at the ready an entire dictionary of words. Any human player that cannot commit to their own mental memory an entire dictionary of words is obviously at a disadvantage.

It is not necessarily an insurmountable disadvantage since, as I've already mentioned, simply knowing about the spelling of all of the possible words is not all that it takes to play the game well. You could have memorized all words in the dictionary and still lose a match due to inadequate strategy. You could even have all those words memorized and play a topnotch strategy, and still lose due to the skills of your opponent and/or due to the luck-of-the-draw in terms of the letters being randomly drawn from the bag.

There is also the time factor involved. A player that can assess more possibilities in the length of time allowed per move is presumably going to have a greater chance of making a better move than otherwise if they could not examine as many options. This limit applies to the human player and their mental processing, and likewise to the AI and its use of computer cycles for processing.

Of course, the depth of mental processing is not necessarily the winning approach since it could be that there are lots of possibilities that aren't worth the mental effort, and nor time, when figuring out your next move.

In short, just because the computer can have at-the-ready an entire dictionary of words does not ergo mean it is going to win. Likewise, even if the AI has an algorithm that uses all kinds of short-cuts and statistics to try and ascertain the seemingly most prudent choice, there is still room for improvement in those algorithms.

This is not a done deal and should not be construed as such.

When considering Scrabble, we might also want to take into account the role of "understanding" when it comes to playing this popular game.

I've already indicated that the non-French speaking winner did not "understand" the words that he was using while playing the French version of Scrabble. Overall, he had no idea what those words meant. They were scratches of lines and curves. These words were icons or images. They were blobs.

That's a good match for using a computer system since the computer and the AI do not "understand" things in the way that we assume humans do.

In playing Scrabble, any player, whether human or AI, does not need to "understand" the words since those are only being used as objects. Any circumstance involving long lists of objects is likely to give the computer a potential advantage since it can presumably have those in computer memory whereas a human is less likely to be able to do so in their own mind. Having a photographic memory by a human would certainly be an exception, though we need to realize there aren't many humans that seem to have a photographic memory.

Now that we've carved out any need for "understanding" in terms of the dictionary of words used in Scrabble, we need to acknowledge the perhaps hidden form of "understanding" needed during the playing of the game. The strategies and tactics used would be applicable to what we commonly refer to as having an "understanding" of something. We don't know for sure what goes on in the heads of a Scrabble player and can only guess at what they might be thinking during the playing of a game.

You can of course ask a Scrabble player what they were thinking. They will tell you what they believe they were thinking. We don't know that it is the same thing as what they were really thinking. It could be a made-up rationalization. If you ask me what I was thinking about during a Scrabble game, and if I don't want you to believe that I was playing the game by some oddball means, I might tell you that I carefully examined the board, I mentally calculated the points, and I thoughtfully determined my next move. I could sincerely "believe" that's what my mind was doing.

We don't know that to be the case. Your mind might be using some other approach entirely. It might seem logical the way you describe it, but that doesn't make it so.

The AI algorithms and techniques employed in the Scrabble playing of Maven and Quackle are maybe similar to what happens in the human mind or maybe not. I'd dare say, most likely probably not. We have come up with some fascinating mathematical and computational approaches that appear to be useful and can compete against humans in a game such as Scrabble.

Does this mean that those AI systems "understand" the game of Scrabble? You'd be hard pressed to say yes.

This is reminiscent of the famous Chinese Room argument. For anyone involved in AI, you ought to be familiar with the thought experiment known as the Chinese Room.

It goes like this. We develop something we regard as AI which we'll place into a room and that can take-in Chinese characters as input and will emit Chinese characters as output, doing so in a manner that a human that is feeding the Chinese characters as input and is reading the Chinese characters of output is led to believe that the AI is a human being. In that sense, this AI passes the infamous Turing Test.

The Turing Test is the notion that if you have a computer and a human, and another human asks questions of the two, when the inquiring human cannot differentiate the computer versus the human, the computer is considered as having passed the Turing Test. It therefore would seem that the computer is able to express intelligence as a human can.

Is the AI that's inside that Chinese room able to "understand" in the same manner that we ascribe the notion of being able to "understand" things as people do?

You could ask that same question of the Turing Test, but the twist somewhat with the Chinese Room is the added element that I will describe next.

Suppose we put an actual human into this Chinese Room. They do not understand a word of Chinese. We also give to the human the same computer program that embodies the AI system. This human endeavors to do exactly what the computer program does, following each instruction explicitly, perhaps using paper and pencil to do so. Notice that the AI is not going to be doing the processing per se, and instead the human inside the Chinese Room will be doing so, following carefully step-by-step whatever the AI would have done.

Presumably, the human inside the Chinese Room is going to once again be able to take-in the Chinese characters as input and emit Chinese characters as output, which we assume will occur due to abiding strictly by the steps of the already-successful AI and be able to convince the human outside the room that the room contains intelligence.

The human in the Chinese room does not understand a word of Chinese, and yet has been able to respond to a Chinese inquirer as though they did understand Chinese, even though it was a "trick" because the human merely followed "mindlessly" the steps indicated of the AI program.

It is claimed that this showcases that there was no real sense of "understanding" involved by the AI and nor by the human that was inside the Chinese room.

Some define the possibility of "strong AI" to be AI that does have a sense of "understanding," while so-called "weak AI" does not and is merely some kind of simulated version of what we refer to as a sense of understanding. The Chinese Room thought experiment is intended to highlight the nature of "weak AI" and do so by way of illustration (which simultaneously also highlights what we consider to not be "strong AI").

Readers should be aware that not everyone accepts the definitions of weak AI and strong AI in this manner. For example, some would say that weak AI is an AI system that might be brittle and easily fooled or confused, while strong AI is an AI system that is more robust and hardier. I hope it is apparent that the use of "weak AI" and "strong AI" in the context of the Chinese Room is quite a different matter of how that vocabulary is used.

A philosopher named John Searle proposed the Chinese Room thought experiment, doing so in 1980, and ever since then there has been quite a response to it. There are lots of arguments about alleged loopholes and fallacies in the thought experiment and this Chinese Room notion. Some critics decry the Chinese Room. Whether you refute it, love it, hate it, despise it, or even believe it is a waste or time, or believe it is a hallmark of thinking about thinking, it has become a longstanding point of discussion and some would consider it a classic of cognitive science and of AI.

I'm not going to tackle the Chinese Room aspects herein. Instead, I bring it up to highlight my earlier point about the playing of Scrabble. I had indicated that it is unknown as to what it means to have "understanding" when it comes to the strategies and tactics of playing Scrabble. We can put to the side any sense of "understanding" about the words used in the Scrabble game, since those are merely objects and in that manner we could claim they are minimal in terms of having to "understand" what they are.

But what about the Scrabble game playing? The AI program of Maven and Quackle, do they embody a sense of "understanding" about the playing of Scrabble, akin to when a human has "understanding" as they play the game?

Most would agree that those AI programs do not have any "understanding" in them.

They are the same then as the Chinese Room.

You might be wondering whether Machine Learning or Deep Learning could maybe rescue us in this situation.

Typically, a Machine Learning or Deep Learning approach involves the use of a large-scale artificial neural network. It is somewhat based on the same aspects of how the human brain perhaps operates, incorporating the use of neurons, synapses, and so on. Today's artificial neural networks are a far cry of being anything close to what happens in the wetware, the human brain. As such, it is at best a simplistic simulation of those biological and biochemical aspects of the brain.

In any case, the assumption and future hope is that if we can keep making computer-based artificial neural networks more and more akin to the human brain, possibly we will have human intelligence emerge in these artificial neural networks. Maybe it won't happen all at once and instead appear in drips and drabs. Maybe it won't ever appear. Maybe there is a secret sauce of the operation of the brain that we'll never be able to crack open. Who knows?

There haven't been many attempts to play Scrabble via the use of an artificial neural network.

The more straight-ahead methods of using various AI search space techniques and algorithms has been the predominant approach used. It seems to make sense that you would use these more overt or symbolic types of approaches, doing a direct kind of programming to solve the problem, rather than using a neural network, which is more of a bottoms-up approach rather than a top-down approach.

With an artificial neural network, it's not quite clear how to best train the neural network for the Scrabble game. Usually, you feed tons of examples or in this case game plays, and the attempt to train the neural network to how the game is played. This in a sense provides a mathematical means to have the artificial neural network do pattern matching and "discover" in a numeric way the strategies and tactics played. This approach has been used in other games such as chess.

If you ponder the difference between a game like chess and a game like Scrabble, you'd readily notice some key attributes that make them very different. In chess, all of the playing pieces are known and placed on the board at the start of the game. In the case of Scrabble, the letters are hidden in a bag and you are dealt out a subset at a time, therefore you have imperfect information and you are also going to be dependent upon random chance of what will occur during the game.

Collecting together a massive number of chess games and being able to feed those as data into an artificial neural network is somewhat easy task to be undertaken. Doing the same for Scrabble games is not so easily done. Even if you do this, the idea of pattern matching based on those games is going to be quite unlike the pattern matching of a chess game.

Here's the rub. If you believe that the use of Machine Learning or Deep Learning is our best shot at achieving human intelligence via AI, presumably we should be using Machine Learning or Deep Learning on trying to craft better and better Scrabble playing automation.

At this time, it would seem that our progress on Machine Learning or Deep Learning is not far enough along to merit believing that the existing employment of Machine Learning or Deep Learning (as we know if it today) would surpass the more direct and programmatic versions of AI such as Maven and Quackle. Perhaps at some future time, this will shift toward the Machine Learning or Deep Learning side of things.

Here's another thought to consider. Are the Machine Learning and Deep Learning systems of today able to "understand" in the same manner that we assume that humans can "understand" things? You'd be hard pressed to have any reasonable AI developer say yes.

If that's the case that these Machine Learning and Deep Learning systems of today are not able to "understand" (in a human sense of "understanding"), will they at some future point be able to do so? Will it be because they become so large-scale in size that "understanding" arises out of the sheer magnitude? Or, will we be doing something else with these models that takes them closer and closer to the true wetware of the human brain?

What does this have to do with AI self-driving cars?

At the Cybernetic AI Self-Driving Car Institute, we are developing AI software for self-driving cars. One aspect that is not widely realized involves the lack of "understanding" that the AI of self-driving cars of today embody and whether that poses safety and risks that aren't being well-discussed.

Allow me to elaborate.

I'd like to first clarify and introduce the notion that there are varying levels of AI self-driving cars. The topmost level is considered Level 5. A Level 5 self-driving car is one that is being driven by the AI and there is no human driver involved. For the design of Level 5 self-driving cars, the auto makers are even removing the gas pedal, brake pedal, and steering wheel, since those are contraptions used by human drivers. The Level 5 self-driving car is not being driven by a human and nor is there an expectation that a human driver will be present in the self-driving car. It's all on the shoulders of the AI to drive the car.

For self-driving cars less than a Level 5, there must be a human driver present in the car. The human driver is currently considered the responsible party for the acts of the car. The AI and the human driver are co-sharing the driving task. In spite of this co-sharing, the human is supposed to remain fully immersed into the driving task and be ready at all times to perform the driving task. I've repeatedly warned about the dangers of this co-sharing arrangement and predicted it will produce many untoward results.

Let's focus herein on the true Level 5 self-driving car. Much of the comments apply to the less than Level 5 self-driving cars too, but the fully autonomous AI self-driving car will receive the most attention in this discussion.

Here's the usual steps involved in the AI driving task:
- Sensor data collection and interpretation
- Sensor fusion
- Virtual world model updating
- AI action planning
- Car controls command issuance

Another key aspect of AI self-driving cars is that they will be driving on our roadways in the midst of human driven cars too. There are some pundits of AI self-driving cars that continually refer to a utopian world in which there are only AI self-driving cars on the public roads. Currently there are about 250+ million conventional cars in the United States alone, and those cars are not going to magically disappear or become true Level 5 AI self-driving cars overnight.

Indeed, the use of human driven cars will last for many years, likely many decades, and the advent of AI self-driving cars will occur while there are still human driven cars on the roads. This is a crucial point since this means that the AI of self-driving cars needs to be able to contend with not just other AI self-driving cars, but also contend with human driven cars. It is easy to envision a simplistic and rather unrealistic world in which all AI self-driving cars are politely interacting with each other and being civil about roadway interactions. That's not what is going to be happening for the foreseeable future. AI self-driving cars and human driven cars will need to be able to cope with each other.

Returning to the topic at-hand, I've been discussing the nature of Scrabble and how humans and how AI systems embody or do not embody a sense of "understanding" in the meaning of what we believe humans can think about things.

When a human drives a car, do you believe that the human is employing "understanding" in some manner, such as understanding how a car operates, understanding how traffic flows and cars maneuver in traffic, and how humans drive cars, and how humans as pedestrians act when near cars, etc.?

If you say yes, this next question is then prompted by the Scrabble discussion and the Chinese Room discussion, namely, will the AI of self-driving cars need to also embody a similar sense of "understanding" in order to properly, safely, and appropriately be driving cars on our public roadways?

Yes or no?

Caught you!

I say that I caught you because if you say yes, and you are of the belief that the AI of self-driving cars needs to have a sense of "understanding" about driving as humans do, right now the auto makers and tech firms are not anywhere close to achieving "understanding" in these AI systems. Simply stated, the AI of today's and even near-future AI self-driving cars do not embody "understanding" at all.

The AI of today's and the near-future self-driving cars is akin to the Scrabble game AI. By-and-large, most of the AI being used in an AI self-driving car is the programmatic type that uses various AI techniques and algorithms, but it is not what we would reasonably agree is any kind of "understanding" that is going on.

You might right away be claiming that since the AI of self-driving cars is often making use of Machine Learning and Deep Learning, it suggests that perhaps the AI is getting closer to having "understanding" in the manner that deep artificial neural networks might someday invoke.

Problematically, those neural networks of today are not yet far advanced toward what someday we all hope might happen with extremely large-scale neural networks and ones that are more closely modeled with the human brain. Furthermore, the neural networks aspects are currently just a small part of the AI stack for self-driving cars.

The use of Deep Learning or Machine Learning is primarily used in the sensors portion of the AI systems for self-driving cars. This makes sense when you consider the duties of the AI subsystems involved in the sensor portion of the driving task. The sensors collect a ton of data. This might be images from the cameras, this might be radar data, LIDAR data, ultrasonic data, and so on.

It is a ready-made situation to use Machine Learning or Deep Learning. We can for example beforehand collect lots of images of street signs. Those can be used to train an artificial neural network. We can then put into the on-board self-driving car system the runnable neural network that will examine an image of a street scene and hopefully be able to detect where a street sign is, along with classifying what kind of street sign it found, such as a Stop sign or a Caution sign.

The AI of the self-driving car does not "understand" the street signs, at least not in the manner that we might believe a human has such an understanding. The street sign is merely an object, akin to the tiles on the Scrabble board of letters that are lines and curves. The rest of the AI has to then use various algorithms and techniques to ascertain what those blobs signify in terms of the action that the self-driving cars should undertake. This would be similar to the Scrabble playing AI that uses various techniques to undertake the strategies and tactics of the game.

As I've repeatedly stated in my writings and presentations, the AI of self-driving cars does not have any common-sense reasoning capability. I mention this because many would say that the act of "understanding" must involve having common sense reasoning. If that indeed is an essential and inseparable ingredient for being able to understand, the sad news is that we are very far away from having any kind of truly robust common-sense reasoning systems.

In essence, we are for now going to be foregoing having AI that has any semblance of human "understanding" and furthermore this applies to the AI of self-driving cars.

When I earlier stated that I caught you, my question had been purposely posed to ask whether or not you thought that AI self-driving cars must have some semblance of human "understanding" to be able to properly and appropriately drive a car on our roadways.

The catch was that if you say yes, well, there then shouldn't be any AI self-driving cars on our roadways as yet.

If you say no to that question, you are then expressing a willingness to have AI that is less-than whatever human "understanding" consists of, and you are suggesting that you are comfortable with that kind of AI being able to drive on our roadways.

This brings me back to another earlier point too. I had mentioned that some AI developers falsely seem to believe that Scrabble has been "solved" as an AI problem. I presume that you now know that though progress has been made, there is still much room to go before we could somehow declare that AI has conquered Scrabble. The aspect that there are in existence some AI programs that can best a human, some of the time, would not seem to be a suitable way to plant a flag and say that the AI that has done so is the best that can be done.

It would hopefully be apparent that I am aiming to say the same thing about the AI for self-driving cars.

We are going to inextricably end-up with this version 1.0 of AI self-driving cars. Let's assume and hope that they are able to drive on our roadways and do so safely (that's a loaded word and one that can mean different things to different people!).

Will that mean that we've conquered the task of driving a car? Some might want to say yes, but I beg to differ. I'm betting that we are going to be able to greatly improve on that version 1.0, and reach a version 2.0, perhaps 3.0, and so on, each getting better and better at driving a car. This will include doing some things that human drivers do, while also doing some things that human drivers do that they ought not to do when driving a car.

Conclusion

Congratulations to the non-French speaking winner of the French-based Scrabble tournament. Just to say, I would be offering the same congratulations if it was a non-English speaking French player that was able to win the English-speaking North American tournament. Winning a Scrabble competition at the topmost level is a feat of incredible strategy and thinking.

I have used the Scrabble aspects as a means to draw your attention to the nature of "understanding" in the matter of human thinking. Per the Chinese Room, we appear to be still at a great distance in today's AI of reaching to any kind of "understanding" that we might agree exists in humans. Whether you like the Chinese Room exemplar or not, it provides another means to bring up the importance of thinking about thinking and trying to figure out what "understanding" actually entails.

For AI self-driving cars, they are coming along, regardless of AI having not yet cracked the secrets of how to achieve the "understanding" that humans have. We are going to presumably accept the notion that we will have AI systems, minus "understanding" which will be driving around cars on our public roadways.

Can those presumed non-understanding AI systems be proficient enough to warrant driving multi-ton cars that will be making human-related life-and-death decisions at every moment as they zip along our streets and highways? Time will tell. Meanwhile, if we do get there, don't fall into the mental trap that the matter has been solved and that there is no AI left to yet be further attained. I assure you, there will be plenty of AI roadway left to be driven and plenty of opportunity for AI developers and researchers in doing so. Hey, the word "opportunity" is an 11-letter word, I wonder if that will fit during my next Scrabble game.

.

CHAPTER 6

COGNITIVE DISORDERS
AND
AI SELF-DRIVING CAR

CHAPTER 6

COGNITIVE DISORDERS

AND

AI SELF-DRIVING CAR

There are an estimated 1 in 5 of adults that will experience a mental illness or mental disorder in a given year (that's based on U.S. statistics, about 20% or around 44 million adults so impacted). Generally, those adults are able to still function sufficiently and continue to operate seemingly "normally" in society. In terms of a quite serious and life altering mental disorder or mental illness that is more debilitating, such a more substantive and deep cognitive impairment will occur to about 1 in 25 of American adults during their life time (that's about 4% or nearly 10 million adults).

That is a lot of people. These are rather staggering numbers when you consider the sheer magnitude of the matter and how many humans are being impacted. Not only are those individuals themselves impacted, so too are the other people around them. The odds are that there is a sizable spillover of a particular individual having a mental disorder or mental illness and it causing loved ones and even strangers to be impacted too.

There's a well-known guide that describes various mental disorders and mental illnesses, known as the DSM (Diagnostic and Statistical Manual of Mental Disorders). I mention the DSM because I sometimes get a reaction from people that seem to think the topic of mental illness or mental disorder is merely when you don't feel like going to work that day or maybe are in a foul mood. It's a lot more than that.

The types of mental disorders or mental illness that I'm referring to consist of schizophrenia, dementia, bipolar disorder, PTSD (Posttraumatic Stress Disorder), anorexia nervosa, autism spectrum disorder, and so on. These are all ailments that can dramatically impact your cognitive capabilities. In some instances the illness or disorder might be relatively mild, while in other case it can be quite severe. You can also at times swing into and out of some of these disorders, appearing to have gotten over one and yet it still lingers and can resurface.

Evolutionary psychologists ask a fundamental and intriguing question about these mental disorders and mental illnesses, namely, why do they exist?

An evolutionary psychologist specializes in the study of how the mind has evolved over time. Similar to others that consider the role of evolution, it is interesting and useful to consider how the brain and the mind have evolved over time. We know based on Darwin's theory of evolution that presumably humans and animals have evolved based on a notion of survival of the fittest.

For whatever traits you might have, if it gives you a leg up on survival, you will tend to procreate and pass along those traits, while others that aren't as strong a fit to the environment will be dying off and thus not passing along those traits. It is not necessarily that the physically strongest people per se will survive, and instead how good a fit they have to the environment that they confront that dictates survival.

This aspect about fit involves not just the physical matters of your body and limbs, but also includes your mental capacities too.

Someone that might be very physically strong could be a poor fit for an environment where being cunning is a crucial element to survival. Suppose I am able to figure out how to make an igloo and can withstand harsh cold weather, while someone much physically stronger is not as clever and tries to live off the snowy landscape without any protective cove or housing. The physically stronger people are likely to die off, while the clever igloo makers won't die off, and therefore those traits of cleverness would be passed along from generation to generation.

You can be a studier of evolution and aim at understanding how the human body and brain have physically evolved over time. Did we at an earlier time period have a body that was fatter or thinner, maybe shorter or taller, perhaps fingers with more dexterity or less dexterity. Did we have a brain that was larger or smaller, and did it have more neurons or less neurons, was it physically the same shape or different than the shape of our brains today. These are primarily physical manifestations of evolution.

What about our minds?

Did we think the same way in the past as we do today? Were we able to think faster or slower? Could we mentally conjure up the complex thoughts that we can today, such as the mental efforts needed for Einstein's theory of relativity or were our predecessors not able to think such in-depth thoughts?

Trying to study the physical elements of human and animal evolution is somewhat straightforward due to the physical evidence of our past. You can generally find the bones of our predecessors and deduce their physical characteristics. You can look at the huts they made and other tools they crafted, providing an indication of what their physical size and condition might have been.

It is a bit more challenging to figure out how our minds have evolved. The emergence of writing and the written record provide a significant clue to our mental capacities, though some would argue that it is not an entirely revealing form of evolutionary evidence. You could also look at the kinds of structures we have built and perhaps use that to guess at how our minds were working at the time, though we would have been limited too by the resources available.

Could you have written a computer program in the 1600's or 1700s? Well, kind of hard to do since there weren't the computer systems that we have today or in modern times. Would the mind of those that were living in that age have been able to write the programs that we can do today? You might assume that of course they could have and argue that all they needed was a Mac or PC or maybe Python or Java to do so.

We know that the abacus seemed to exist in the time of Babylon, and so you could infer that we had a mental capacity at that time for computing of a kind. There are historians that say the Greeks had a mechanical analog device, perhaps we'll call it a computer, known as the Antikythera mechanism. This Greek "computer" was able to enhance calendars and served to improve astronomical predictions such as the appearance of eclipses.

In any case, you might have always assumed that the thinking that we do today is the same as the thinking of earlier humans, but we don't know that's the case for sure. Some people say that our minds are like vessels and the vessels have always been the same, while it is just the content that differs. In modern times, we have different content than did they have available in Babylon and for the Greeks. Nonetheless, you might argue that they still had the same thinking and mental capabilities as we do today.

This might not be the case. It could be that our mental capabilities have evolved over time. Perhaps our mental processing was of a more limited nature in the past. It could be that our ability to think has gotten better and better.

One also needs to be careful to not unnecessarily try to separate out the physical aspects from the mental aspects of thinking. In other words, the size and shape of the brain, it's physical characteristics, might have something to do with our capacity to think. As such, as the brain has physically changed over time, which is relatively easier to document and detect, so too would presumably our ability to think.

You might try to argue that no matter what the physical characteristics of the human brain are, we are still able to think the same way and come up with the same thoughts. This seems like a doubtful theory. If we take a look at what we know of ancient cave dwellers, and the nature of their physical brains, it sure seems unlikely they could have had the same kind of thinking powers that we have today.

I am dragging you through this discussion about the brain versus the mind and do so to get us to the question posed by evolutionary psychologists.

Why do we have mental disorders or mental illnesses?

Tying this to the aspects of evolution, one might assert that if mental illnesses and mental disorders are a bad thing, which I would guess most people would agree is likely the case, shouldn't we have mentally evolved in a manner that those mental disorders or mental illnesses would no longer exist today?

Going back to my earlier example about the igloo, let's recast the matter into the case of those that are prone to mental disorders versus those that are not. If we had a population of people and there was a segment that tended to have mental disorders, and another segment of people that tended to not have mental disorders, over time and the gradual exorcising aspects of survival of the fittest, it would seem that we'd expect those with mental disorders to not be surviving. They should no longer be passing along their mental disorder genes. Meanwhile, those that aren't prone to mental disorders should be surviving and passing along their "no mental disorders" genes.

Gradually, the population should no longer exhibit mental disorders, one would theorize. It's an evolutionary psychological phenomenon, we might suppose. Yet, as I mentioned earlier, around 20% of adults will have a mental disorder in a given year, and around 4% will have a debilitating and substantive mental disorder in their lifetime. Doesn't seem like evolution has led to the eradication of mental disorders.

One argument is that those 20% and 4% numbers are perhaps pretty good. Maybe hundreds of years ago it was more like 50% and 10%, and we've gradually had evolution winding down on those percentages. Perhaps we should be pleased to see that it is "only" the 20% and 4% today, and we might also then anticipate or predict that in a few more hundreds of years it will continue to winnow.

Another argument is that maybe we will always see numbers of around 20% and 4% respectively. It could be that our mental processing is going to have mental disorders, no matter what else happens. In a sense, the advent of mental disorders is a kind of rounding error. If you want to have our grandiose capabilities of thinking, you need to accept that a certain percentage of the time there are going to be mental disorders. It is the yin and yang of having mental capacities.

Yet another argument is that we still in the midst of mental evolution and we don't really know what is yet going to happen about our mental capacities. Maybe, in some weird way, we are going to evolve toward having even much higher percentages of mental disorders. It could be that those with the mental disorders are tending toward survival, while those without mental disorders will not. In this kind of bizarro world order, the 20% and 4% is someday going to be 90% and 70% (or other overwhelming counts).

You could tag along on the rising tide of mental disorder by theorizing that if there is a rounding error of having highly tuned mental capacities, the smarter we get then maybe the more of a rounding error that appears. That's another vote then for the potential of having more mental disorders rather than having less.

We might need to also add into this evolutionary equation our own efforts regarding mental disorders.

I've so far acted as though evolution just happens and there isn't any kind of human led impact on how things might evolve. Some would argue that we humans can shape to a significant extent how we evolve. For example, there is the couch potato theory that if we aren't going outside and exercising as much as we used to do, the human body will evolve towards those bodies that are suited for couch potato efforts, apparently playing video games and doing binge watching of online cat videos (hint: we'll have slovenly bodies!).

There are lots of efforts afoot to try and treat mental disorders. Likewise, there are efforts underway to prevent mental disorders from arising. Could those human led efforts thusly impact the evolutionary elements of mental disorders?

Some say that mental disorders will remain in our DNA and yet will be suppressed by these human led efforts. The potential of having a mental disorder will remain underground, hidden within our minds, and the human led efforts will merely keep it from springing forth. In that sense, we'll supposedly continue to have the same mental disorder capacities as we do now, but the numbers of those exhibiting it will shrink.

Others would say that we are going to figure out what leads to mental disorders, somewhat akin to finding the source of the Nile. Once we figure out the basis for mental disorders, we'll be able to trigger them off (or, I suppose, on), via specialized drugs or other means. It could be a physical brain aspect that's involved. Or, it might be a purely "thinking" aspect and that by a specialized form of meditation you can prevent mental disorders. Someone might discover a universal mantra that when said repeatedly gets the mind to veer away from mental disorder. Who knows?

You could potentially argue that we need to have mental disorders or mental illnesses, since they might be a helpful sign and we just don't realize it is. Perhaps it is like a mental alarm clock. The mental disorder is forewarning that the mind of the person is having difficulties. The mental disorder is like showcasing a fever when your body is starting to get sick. The fever gets your attention and you then take other efforts to help fight a bodily infection.

If we are going to suppress mental disorders, it could knock down our chances of detecting when someone's overall mind is maybe beginning to tilt. Without the early warning system of the emergence of the mental disorder, perhaps their entire mind is going to break like an egg. If you suppress a fever and don't know that a fever exists, you aren't able to take other measures to get the body ready for the infection or illness that's trying to take over the body. Same might be said about the mind.

Does a mental disorder imply that our minds are fragile and brittle?

Some would say that it is such a sign. Others might claim that it is actually a robust kind of signal, allowing the mind to let us know when something is amiss. We just don't know today that it is that kind of signal and nor what to do about it. Down the road, once we've cracked the enigma of thinking, perhaps we'll realize that mental disorders were a means to ascertain when a mind needed tuning. We just didn't have the wherewithal to know what the sign meant and nor the tuning forks in-hand to deal with it.

There's also the aggregate versus individual perspective.

Perhaps as a population, as a society, we need to have some percentage of humans that have a mental disorder. This seems at first glance nonsensical. We assume that all mental disorders should be erased or removed from society.

We don't know what society would be like if we did so. You could claim that society would be better off, and we'd no longer have members of the population that are seemingly abnormal in comparison to the rest of the mental status of the population.

Maybe we need to have a certain proportion of the society that has a mental disorder or mental illness. Without it, the society perhaps becomes worse off. Our societal capacity might be undermined if we eliminated all mental disorders, some might argue.

I'd like to leave you there for the moment, regarding the matter of mental disorders as it relates to evolutionary psychology, and let you ruminate about it.

Let's now shift our attention to Artificial Intelligence (AI).

Here's why. If you believe that mental disorders or mental illness is an essential ingredient of thinking, and if AI is hoping to create a form of automation that is the equivalent of human thinking, should AI be incorporating "mental disorders" into AI systems?

When I pose this question, there are some AI developers that immediately gag and start to upchuck their lunch or midday snacks. Say, what? Are you serious, they ask?

These AI developers are striding mightily to make their AI systems as "perfect" as possible. Their vaunted goal is flawlessness. That's the sacred quest for nearly every AI developer and software engineer on this planet. The system they develop needs to work without errors. It isn't easy to achieve. It is very hard to achieve. We don't even know if it possible to have flawless AI systems.

The radical notion that the AI systems should intentionally have "mental disorders" is a kind of high treason statement. It is the antithesis of what developers are trying to do. Oh, so we can not only allow errors to accidently creep into our systems, they say, but we are now supposed to actually build into those systems an on-purpose dysfunctional aspect? It is truly a sign of the apocalypse; some AI developers would lament.

Well, not so fast with those cries of foul.

Perhaps to reach true intelligence we might need to mix both the good and the bad of human mental processing. Suppose those two are inextricably linked. You might not be able to have the good, if you don't also have the bad.

In that case, all of these AI efforts are doomed to not actually reach true intelligence, since they are intentionally avoiding and trying to prevent the bad. Simply stated, no bad, then ultimately no true emergence of the good aspects of intelligence. You might hit a barrier above which automated AI systems will never get any higher up the intelligence spectrum.

Notice too that I've fallen somewhat into the trap of labelling the mental disorders or mental illnesses as "bad," which might be an inappropriate categorization. As mentioned earlier, it could be that mental disorders or mental illnesses serve a useful and "good" purpose, but we just don't yet realize this to be the case. By taking the simplistic route of labeling it as bad, it lulls us into wanting to disregard it, and get us to expunge it.

This seems to be an advocacy for intentional imperfection, assuming you are tossing mental disorders into the strictly "bad" classification.

Let's pursue this logic about the potential need for "mental disorders" in AI systems. If you are interacting with an AI system that is using Natural Language Processing (NLP), you would presumably want the AI to interact with you in a completely fluent and mentally stable way. Suppose it suddenly sparked a moment of schizophrenia during the dialogue with a human. Most of us are familiar with paranoid schizophrenia, often depicted in movies and TV shows, so we'll use that type for this example.

You are using the AI NLP to place an order for your baseball team via an online sports products catalog. After looking at various baseballs bats and interacting with the NLP about which bats might be best to order, the AI unexpectedly drops into a paranoid schizophrenia episode. Are you getting that bat to hurt someone, it asks? Maybe to come and hurt me, it queries of the human. I'd guess that you might be disturbed by this line of questioning and opt to order your baseball gear from another web site that doesn't have an AI system containing paranoia tendencies.

Okay, so that seems to showcase that maybe we don't want AI to embody mental disorders.

I'll though return to the earlier point that maybe we won't be able to achieve true AI systems without there also being present the potential for mental disorders. In that case, it then becomes an added factor of making sure that the AI system is able to self-check itself and catch the mental disorder before it emerges in a manner that is unsettling or creates problems. In the baseball bat example, there might be a self-check that catches the NLP as it attempts to ask the paranoid-like questions, and stops the AI from doing so, avoiding the rather disturbing impact it might have on the interacting human.

I'll try to make this even more seemingly "sensible" by going the route of error handling in AI systems.

Do you believe that your AI system is utterly error free? If you say yes, I'd like to suggest you either have a toy-sized AI system that has no real complexity, or you are delusional (mental disorder!) about what your AI system is or might do.

Hopefully, most reasonable AI developers would acknowledge that there is a chance that an error exists within their AI system. A reasonable chance and not a zero chance. It might be entirely there by accident. It might be there by some intentional act. In any case, yes, there's a chance or probability that an error or errors exist in the AI system.

Sadly, many AI developers don't do much toward trying to catch errors. They focus most of their attention on trying to debug their systems for errors, and once they've finished the debugging, they release the AI system and hope that there aren't errors as yet unfound. They tend to not build into the executing system itself much in the way of being able to catch errors as they arise at run time.

In theory, there should be a robust error detecting capability of any well-built and well-engineered AI system.

This is especially needed for AI systems that might involve serious consequences due to any hidden errors that might be encountered. An AI robotic arm in a manufacturing plant might go awry due to a hidden error or bug, and could potentially harm humans that are nearby, or cause destruction to the facilities of the manufacturing plant.

So, here's where I am taking you. If we can agree that an AI system ought to have some definitive and robust error detection capabilities, we might dovetail into this notion and say that if "mental disorders" are needed to achieve truly intelligent systems, we can abide by that assertion, and still be hopefully be protected by ensuring that the otherwise already-needed error detection capability can cover for whatever untoward action that the "mental disorder" portion might cause.

Admittedly, I'd be quite hesitant at this stage of our collective understanding of the purpose for mental disorders or mental illnesses in humans, and the role it plays in intelligence, for me to be saying that you ought to willy nilly be adding such aspects into your AI system, and simultaneously trying to curtail or remedy them those mental disorders or mental illnesses via an enhanced error processing capability.

Perhaps this is more a future looking kind of approach. Down the road, assume we get stuck trying to achieve true AI, and are unsure of why. We scratch our heads, baffled because we've seemingly tried everything that would make "sense" to try and do. Counter-intuitively, the secret sauce it turns out is that we forgot to include mental disorders (well, perhaps we didn't forget to do so, and instead intentionally avoided doing so), and so now to get to the final level of intelligence we need to add those into our AI systems.

Here's another twist for you.

First, be aware that there are two major camps of how we'll achieve true AI.

One camp is the bottoms-up approach that tends to emphasize the Machine Learning or Deep Learning ways of developing an AI system. Typically using a large-scale or deep artificial neural network, this approach is essentially trying to mimic how the brain physically seems to be composed. We don't yet really know the manner in which thinking arises from the trillions of neurons and quadrillions of synapses in the human brain, but maybe we'll get lucky in that the efforts to simulate the brain via computational power and artificial neural networks will get us to true AI.

For the other camp, referred to often as the tops-down or symbolist group, the approach consists of pretty much programming our way toward true AI. Rather than trying to mimic the physical attributes of the human brain, we might be able to logically figure out what thinking consists of, and then create it in automation without having to essentially duplicate a brain structure per se.

The top-down camp would likely decry the bottoms-up approach and suggest that it might or might not lead to true AI, but if it does reach true AI, we might not know how it did so. We are only creating another black box and won't have cracked open its secrets. Fine, say the bottoms-up proponents, since at least we'll be able to use computational power to do what human intelligence can do, and maybe we don't need to know how or why it happens but we achieved true AI (plus, there is the chance that during the journey to the black box we might actually unlock its secrets).

The bottoms-up camp might likely decry that the tops-down approach might not ever logically deduce how intelligence arises and be adrift forever trying to figure it out. It could be something that is not explainable in any manner that we can devise. Perhaps it is going to always be a black box.

Rather than fruitlessly seeking to guess at the myriad of ways in which intelligence might be invented, let's not avoid the one thing we have that has intelligence, the actual human brain.

Ahem, excuse me if I've somewhat overstated the extremity of the camp positions herein, which I do just for illustrative purposes. I'll also offer that these are not necessarily mutually exclusive camps that are at dire and acrimonious logger heads (though some are!), and they can and do often work together (yes, they do). Happy campers at times, one might say.

I'm now getting to the twist that I wanted to share with you and will show how the camps matter ties to the topic of mental disorders and mental illnesses.

As stated, we have two overarching AI-aiming camps, one that is trying to build true AI from the bottoms-up, while the other camp is trying to go the route of top-down.

Suppose the bottoms-up camp discovers that mental disorders or mental illnesses emerge as part of the Machine Learning or Deep Learning neural networks approach. It just happens. Not because the camp made it so. Instead, once the large-scale Machine Learning or Deep Learning gets large enough, perhaps various forms of mental disorders and mental illnesses begin to appear as an outcrop of massively sized artificial neural networks.

This goes along with the notion that possibly our mental processing involving the "good" is inextricably connected with the "bad" (if we are going to label mental disorders as such).

If that "surprising" emergence happens, it would be quite interesting and would force us to reconsider what to do about the mental disorders and mental illnesses, which would then be ascribed as artificial mental disorders and artificial mental illnesses (artificial meaning as arising in the AI).

Meanwhile, let's assume that the other camp, the tops-down advocates, either stumble upon the use of artificial mental disorders, perhaps inadvertently arising from the logics of their AI systems, or decide to purposely include mental disorders, in hopes of seeing whether it boosts overall the true AI attainment. They too might need to cope with the nuances of artificial mental disorders and artificial mental illnesses.

That's some food for thought about the evolution of AI. Whoa, evolution, it's all around us.

An entirely different perspective on this topic overall is that it at least highlights the importance of thinking about how mental disorders and mental illnesses arise in the matter of how we think. Not many in the AI field are giving this much due. As stated earlier, when your goal is aiming at perfection, you might not be carefully studying the nature of "imperfection," but which if you did it might help you toward getting to the perfection that you seek. The yin and the yang, as it were.

Likewise, it is useful to consider what we can learn or glean from human mental disorders and mental illnesses for purposes of building AI systems from an error processing perspective. I'd dare say that the more we put error processing at the forefront of AI development, the better we will all be.

I mention this too because oftentimes it seems that error detection is shouldered solely by an individual AI developer. In my book, it takes a village to properly fight the error detection battle. By this I mean that if you are an individual AI developer and the only one of your team that seems to be devoted to error detection aspects, it is going to be an uphill battle.

You need to have AI leadership and management that embraces the error detection aspects. If the top leaders are only focused on error prevention, they will miss the aspects of error detection, a crucial fail-safe layer to any properly engineered AI system. An individual AI developer might not be provided with the resources, nor the time and rewards, needed to appropriately deal with error detection. In that case, the culture and leadership of the AI team has undermined a vital element of the AI system, and it is oversimplifying to put your gaze solely on the individual AI developer.

What does this have to do with AI self-driving cars?

At the Cybernetic AI Self-Driving Car Institute, we are developing AI software for self-driving cars. Auto makers and tech firms need to be wise to error detection for AI self-driving cars, particularly since the safety of self-driving cars and humans are at stake. Perhaps mulling over the nature of AI and artificial mental disorders will spark such attention.

Allow me to elaborate.

I'd like to first clarify and introduce the notion that there are varying levels of AI self-driving cars. The topmost level is considered Level 5. A Level 5 self-driving car is one that is being driven by the AI and there is no human driver involved. For the design of Level 5 self-driving cars, the auto makers are even removing the gas pedal, brake pedal, and steering wheel, since those are contraptions used by human drivers. The Level 5 self-driving car is not being driven by a human and nor is there an expectation that a human driver will be present in the self-driving car. It's all on the shoulders of the AI to drive the car.

For self-driving cars less than a Level 5, there must be a human driver present in the car. The human driver is currently considered the responsible party for the acts of the car. The AI and the human driver are co-sharing the driving task. In spite of this co-sharing, the human is supposed to remain fully immersed into the driving task and be ready at all times to perform the driving task. I've repeatedly warned about the dangers of this co-sharing arrangement and predicted it will produce many untoward results.

Let's focus herein on the true Level 5 self-driving car. Much of the comments apply to the less than Level 5 self-driving cars too, but the fully autonomous AI self-driving car will receive the most attention in this discussion.

Here's the usual steps involved in the AI driving task:
- Sensor data collection and interpretation
- Sensor fusion
- Virtual world model updating
- AI action planning
- Car controls command issuance

Another key aspect of AI self-driving cars is that they will be driving on our roadways in the midst of human driven cars too. There are some pundits of AI self-driving cars that continually refer to a utopian world in which there are only AI self-driving cars on the public roads. Currently there are about 250+ million conventional cars in the United States alone, and those cars are not going to magically disappear or become true Level 5 AI self-driving cars overnight.

Indeed, the use of human driven cars will last for many years, likely many decades, and the advent of AI self-driving cars will occur while there are still human driven cars on the roads. This is a crucial point since this means that the AI of self-driving cars needs to be able to contend with not just other AI self-driving cars, but also contend with human driven cars. It is easy to envision a simplistic and rather unrealistic world in which all AI self-driving cars are politely interacting with each other and being civil about roadway interactions. That's not what is going to be happening for the foreseeable future. AI self-driving cars and human driven cars will need to be able to cope with each other.

Returning to the topic of mental disorders and mental illnesses, let's see how a focus on cognitive impairments might be useful when trying to build robust and reliable AI self-driving cars.

I'll start by reusing my overall framework about AI self-driving cars, which contains the various overarching elements to be considered about AI self-driving cars. Using a core subset of factors, I've put together an indictor of how the AI might exhibit a diminished capacity if any of the selected factors goes awry.

I refer to this chart as the ABCDEFG, based on the one-word indications that are used to describe each of the seven circumstances.

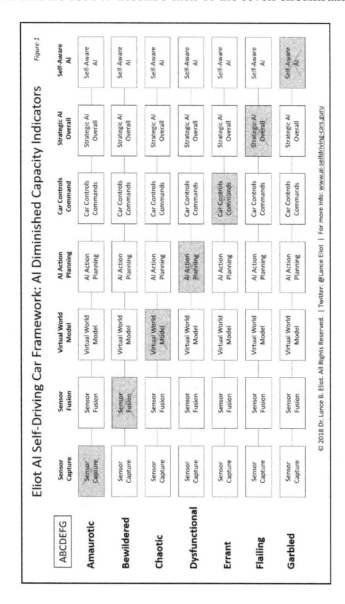

Figure 1

Eliot AI Self-Driving Car Framework: AI Diminished Capacity Indicators

© 2018 Dr. Lance B. Eliot. All Rights Reserved. | Twitter: @Lance Eliot | For more info: www.ai-selfdriving-cars.guru

Let's start with the letter A and the word Amaurotic.

You might not be familiar with the word amaurotic, which means to have lost your vision or from the Greek meaning to be obscured. This is an apt description of an AI self-driving car that might have some kind of "mental disorder" involving the sensors and their data collection.

The sensors of the self-driving car are the means of the AI being able to detect what is taking place surrounding the AI self-driving car. If those sensors aren't working properly, the AI would have an inadequate indication of what is taking place around the self-driving car. A pedestrian might not be spotted that is precariously close to where the self-driving car is currently headed. A car ahead of the self-driving car might be misjudged as accelerating forward when it is actually starting to hit the brakes.

An artificial mental disorder or artificial mental illness, which I'm appending the word "artificial" to connote is it something happening within the automation, could cause the sensors to act incorrectly or be interpreted incorrectly.

Suppose the camera is capturing excellent images, and yet the portion of the AI subsystem that interprets those images is acting incorrectly. You or I might look at the images and clearly be able to see a pedestrian, while the AI subsystem interpreting the image might report that the pedestrian is far away or maybe not even there at all.

Why would the AI subsystem falter in such a manner? It could be that there is some kind of error that has arisen within that AI subsystem. Assuming that there is insufficient error checking to catch it, the AI subsystem might pass along its false interpretation to the rest of the AI overall system that is driving the self-driving car.

That's bad news for the rest of the AI since everything else of the AI self-driving car is taking at face value that the interpretation of the sensory data by the image processing subsystem is working correctly. That's bad news for any human occupants inside the self-driving car, and bad news for any humans nearby the AI self-driving car, since the odds are that the rest of the AI is going to make poor driving decisions based on the faulty reporting by the sensory "mental disorder" that is occurring.

If you want to do so, we can play with the mental disorder vocabulary a little bit.

Suppose a car is coming down the street and will pass right by the AI self-driving car, heading in the opposite direction of the self-driving car. This happens all the time when you are driving, and you typically don't give much attention to a car that is coming toward you in the opposing lane and will presumably go alongside you for a brief instant and then go past you.

When you ponder this for a moment, it is actually remarkable that we allow other cars to zip past us, missing your car by just a few scant feet, doing so on busy highways and freeways, often without anything separating us from complete disaster and striking each other head-on at frighteningly fast speeds, other than a painted line on the street. It should strike terror into us. Instead, we grow numb to the potential for absolute destruction and mayhem.

I recall when my children were first learning to drive that I was at times holding my breath when they drove on busy streets and highways. From the front passenger seat, serving in my role as doting father wanting to help as they became experienced drivers, I couldn't quite tell how close we were going to be when an opposing car came alongside our car. Often, I was sure that we were going to slam head-on and found myself clinching up at the prospects of it. Fortunately, we did not ram into other cars and nor did other cars ram into us.

Again, nationwide and worldwide, I look at this all as a miracle that on a daily basis we don't have thousands upon thousands upon thousands of daily head-on killer crashes.

In any case, suppose an AI self-driving car is driving along and another car in the opposing direction is going to eventually come alongside the self-driving car and pass by it. The sensors of the AI self-driving car would normally be detecting the other car, doing so at some distance prior to the point of near crossing of each other. The camera would be capturing images and video streams, out of which the image processing AI subsystem would be relaying to the rest of the AI system that there is an object approaching at a fast speed, it is a car, and it is predicted to pass alongside.

The rest of the AI would likely then have no need to react to this other car. It's handy to be aware that the other car exists, just in case the AI is trying to determine whether it might be able to use the opposing lane for any upcoming evasive maneuvers that might be otherwise needed. The AI would calculate that the opposing lane is a somewhat risky place now, for the moment, since there's a car coming along in that lane.

Imagine that the image processing starts to hallucinate or become delusional. I am using those words in a loose manner and don't necessarily mean those words in a proper clinical psychological way. In the case of the AI subsystem, let's suppose it has some kind of error or bug and this causes the AI subsystem to categorize the car in the opposing lane as a motorcycle rather than a car. This seems plausible as a result of some internal error.

The error cascades and it causes the AI subsystem that is doing the image interpretation to instead reclassify the "perceived" motorcycle to instead be a dog. This might seem less plausible, but keep in mind that the image processing system likely has lots of classifications for objects that could be detected, including classifying motorized vehicles as to being cars, trucks, motorcycles, etc. Likewise, the classification includes types of animals such as whether a dog is spotted, a cat, a cow, a horse, any of which could be wandering onto a road that the self-driving car might be driving on.

The AI subsystem that has the error is in a manner of speaking delusional in that it now is reporting that an upcoming car is actually a dog.

We can add the hallucination aspect by suggesting that the AI subsystem error also causes it to report that there is a cow and a horse there too, running next to the dog. There isn't any other moving object adjacent to the upcoming car, but the errors inside the automation are so out-of-whack that it is adding objects into the scene that aren't actually there at all.

This provides an example of how an artificial mental disorder or artificial mental illness could impact the AI self-driving car.

If you want to consider the role of paranoia, we could say that the image processing has an error but different than the one so far described. Suppose the AI subsystem is able to ascertain that a car is in the opposing lane. Unfortunately, due to an error, the AI subsystem makes a prediction that the car is going to strike head-on to the AI self-driving car.

Maybe the way in which the passing alongside software routine works is that if there is a clearance of more than 12 inches the flag is set to safe-to-pass, while if the clearance is less than a foot it will set the flag to head-on. Even though in this case the car is really going to pass alongside at a "safe" distance of say 18 inches, an error in the calculation mistakenly calculates the distance to be 8 inches. This then causes the head-on flag to occur. The rest of the AI receives a head-on indication from the image processing interpretation and would presumably react accordingly.

In fact, the routine is now caught up in this error activity. Anything in the opposing lane is going to get flagged as a head-on. That car is flagged as head-on, a bicyclist in the opposing lane is flagged as a head-on, and a pedestrian that is standing at the curb of the opposing lane is flagged as a head-on.

Does the AI seem to now be a bit paranoid? It "thinks" that everyone is out to get it, coming at the self-driving car head-on. Yikes!

I mentioned that I wanted to use the word "artificial" in front of the phrases of mental disorder and mental illness. Part of the reason to do so is due to the aspect that the manner of how various mental disorders arise in the human mind and the brain is still relatively unknown. We seem to be able to discern the behavioral impacts those mental disorders have, yet we aren't exactly sure what gives rise to them.

I want to therefore make sure to distinguish that the AI is suffering from a kind of "mental disorder" that is not necessarily doing so in the same underlying manner that the human brain and mind do. Instead, we're focusing herein on the behavioral results that are similar. By using the word "artificial" I am trying to forewarn that we should not make the logic leap that the AI-based mental disorder is necessarily the same as the human mental disorder aspects in terms of the underlying roots, and instead only on the basis of the behavioral results.

Let's now consider what would happen to the AI self-driving car if the sensor fusion portion suffered from an artificial mental disorder.

I'd say that the result would be a Bewildered system. The sensor fusion is intended to bring together the various sensory interpretations and try to determine how they compare with each other. This means that if the image processing is saying there is a car coming along, and yet the radar does not detect a car there, the sensor fusion must ascertain what conclusion to reach. It's a potentially complex effort to ferret out the consistencies and inconsistencies between the multitude of sensors on the self-driving car and what each is suggesting it has found or not found.

When the sensor fusion is fouled up, it might be falsely claiming that the sensors are in disagreement, when they actually all agree as to what is outside of the self-driving car. Or, the sensor fusion might falsely claim that all the sensors are in agreement, when in fact the sensors are differing in terms of what they have each detected. You might characterize this as a kind of being bewildered and unsure of what the surrounding scene contains.

The next word is Chaotic.

If the virtual world model is suffering from an artificial mental disorder, it won't be able to properly denote where objects in the real-world are. The model is intended to keep track of where objects exist outside of the self-driving car, along with predictions about where those objects are heading. It is kind of like an air traffic control subsystem, wanting to monitor the status of nearby objects.

Imagine if the virtual world modelling subsystem of the AI were to breakdown and start putting objects just anywhere. The car that is in the opposing lane might incorrectly be portrayed as in the same lane as the self-driving car. Or, maybe the pedestrian on the sidewalk is misplaced in the model as though they are standing in the middle of the street.

That would be a chaotic indication.

The word I'd like to cover next is Dysfunctional.

If the AI action planning subsystem of the AI is suffering from an artificial mental disorder, you are going to witness a dysfunctional AI self-driving car. Suppose the sensors are working just fine, the sensor fusion is working just fine, and the virtual world modelling is working just fine. Meanwhile, when the AI action planner inspects the virtual world model, the action planner is messing up and has some form of error in it.

Even though the sensors are reporting that the car in the opposing lane is going to pass alongside safely, and the sensor fusion supports that indication, and the virtual world model clearly states as such, the AI action planner is living in its own dream world. As such, it ignores what those other subsystems have indicated. Thus, maybe the AI action planner decides that it would be best for the AI self-driving car to swerve into the opposing lane, doing so under a false belief that the car in the opposing lane is coming into the existing lane of the AI self-driving car.

This is dysfunctional or worse.

The next word is Errant.

For the car controls commands issuance, this subsystem of the AI is intended to generate instructions to the car as to what it is supposed to physically next do, such as accelerating, braking, and the direction of the steering of the car. Suppose the sensors detected an opposing car that was going to pass alongside safely, the sensor fusion concurred, the virtual world model concurred, the AI action planner concurred, and so up until this point there is no action specified to take.

Unfortunately, if the car controls command issuance is suffering from an artificial mental disorder, it might decide to turn the steering wheel directly into the path of that oncoming car. An error of some kind has inadvertently turned a result from the AI action planner that said to stay straight and instead changed it to adjust the steering wheel for a sharp left maneuver into the opposing lane.

This is errant or worse.

The next word is Flailing.

For the strategic AI elements of the self-driving car, suppose that an artificial mental disorder arose. For example, maybe the AI self-driving car is supposed to be headed to downtown Los Angeles. An error though in the strategic AI elements gets things messed-up and the AI is led toward Las Vegas, Nevada. Maybe the strategic AI is so error laden that it keeps changing where the destination is supposed to be. The self-driving car seems to be changing from one direction to the other, no rhyme or reason apparent as to it doing so.

This is flailing or worse.

The last word to cover is Garbled.

If the self-aware AI aspects aren't able to do a proper effort toward tracking how well the rest of the AI system is working, perhaps due to an artificial mental disorder, it could lead to a garbling of what the AI self-driving car is going to do. One moment the self-aware AI is informing the rest of the AI it is doing well, and the next moment it is warning that one element or another is fouled up.

This is being garbled or worse.

Conclusion

Mental disorders and mental illnesses are a substantial part of the human experience. Why? Evolution might suggest that we should be rid of those aspects by now. Maybe though it is something still being worked out by evolution and we are merely in the middle of things, and therefore cannot say for sure whether those disorders and illnesses will continue or gradually be diminished based on a survival of the fittest path.

Will AI need to include mental disorders or mental illness if indeed those facets are inextricably tied into human intelligence, and perhaps the only means to reach true intelligence is to include those factors? If so, what does it mean about how we are developing AI systems today. Including artificial mental disorders or artificial mental illnesses seems quite counter-intuitive to the usual belief that AI systems need to be free of any such potential downfalls.

It could be that the basis for including artificial mental disorders or artificial mental illnesses is either of merit on its own, or that we can use the basis to then be more circumspect about how AI systems need to cope with internal "cognitive impairments" or internal errors that might arise in the "thinking" elements of the AI system.

Regardless of whether you think it might be preposterous to consider mental disorders or mental illnesses in the context of building AI systems, you might at least be open to the notion that it brings up the importance of making sure AI systems are as error detecting and correcting as they can be.

If we can be somewhat liberal with the use of the terminology of mental disorder and mental illness, and restate it as a form of internal mental errors, and if AI systems are supposed to be crafted on some kind of considered mental processing, we can use this to highlight the importance of individual AI developers taking error handling seriously, and get the AI teams to do the same. It takes a village to cope with the mental disorders and mental illnesses, both of society as a whole and of AI systems in of themselves, and we all need to work on this.

I'd say there's no mental confusion on that key point.

CHAPTER 7

NOISE POLLUTION

ABATEMENT

AND

AI SELF-DRIVING CARS

CHAPTER 7

NOISE POLLUTION ABATEMENT AND AI SELF-DRIVING CARS

I was being serenaded. Standing on the street corner at New York Times Square, I was surrounded by the epic and at times overwhelming sounds of New York City (NYC). I had come to the city that never sleeps to speak at an industry conference on Artificial Intelligence (AI). Opting to walk from my hotel to the conference location, I couldn't help but hear the nefarious noises of this hustling and bustling famous town.

Bang, bam, honk, honk, whoosh, woot, bang, and so on, there was a cacophony of noises coming at me, drowning me in a sea of diverse and often bone-rattling sounds. NYC has a lot of claim to fame, and one of those claims is that it is the noisiest city in all of North America (not just limited to the United States!). I realize that there are other cities that might dispute this claim, though I am not sure that anyone would really want to admit that their city is the grandest of them all due to loud and overbearing noises.

Environmentalists would label it as noise pollution.

Some New Yorkers are proud of the noises that emanate throughout their domain. That loud banging is coming from yet another construction project, consisting of a new skyscraper being built with steel girders and producing a commensurate volume of construction noises. It is a showcase of the growth of the area and the promise of more jobs.

The streets are filled with cars, cabs, buses, motorcyclists, bicyclists, all producing traffic noises, though admittedly the amount of horn honking is nowadays a lot less than it used to be (due to a crackdown on honking incessantly). Many New Yorkers would readily admit that their traffic situation is horrendous and there is a continual plethora of noises coming from the cars, including car exhaust noises, car doors opening and closing noises, tire screeching noises, cars bumping along on potholes noises, cars hitting each other noises, etc.

But, as the locals say, you get used to the sounds. Indeed, some of my colleagues that live in NYC have at times looked at me with a puzzled expression when I mention the noises that I hear when I stay there. The puzzlement is due to the fact that they, as locals, no longer overtly hear the sounds, having become so accustomed to the noises. Usually, when walking with them on the streets of NYC, they'll completely ignore the noises and be chatting with me as though we are walking in a quiet wooded forest and there is nothing that makes any abrasive noises, it is as though we are immersed among the song of gentle birds in a forest or are hearing the sweet sounds of trees gently swaying in the wind.

I assure you that those sounds are not quite so sweet as imagined. You can certainly try to block out the noises of the city, either mentally ignoring them or pretending they are minimal, but nonetheless your ears are getting pounded. Sound is energy.

Typically measured in Sound Pressure Levels (SPLs), those city noises are battering your ears. Often, it is customary to use dBA's (formerly described as A-weighted decibels) as a scale for comparing different kinds of noises. The SPL dBA is a logarithmic scale and you need to carefully interpret the numbers used, realizing that as the numbers increase it is not simply a linear progression.

Let's consider some sounds that pertain to human hearing. The sound of a pin dropping is 10 dBA. You have pretty good ears to ear that sound. Rustling leaves are typically around 20 dBA, while a babbling brook is about 40 dBA. So far, these are all relatively quiet and readily enjoyable sounds.

Your alarm clock that sharply awakens you in the mornings is likely around 80 dBA. That's a sound that is not just jarring, it is also perhaps universally hated because of its significance (yes, a sound meaning it is time to get up and go to work, again!). The sound of a jackhammer gets you to about 110 dBA. A gun being fired is probably 160 dBA or more. Those are rather obnoxious sounds and ones that can cause either temporary damage to your ears or have permanent adverse impacts on your ears.

In a somewhat serene suburbia, the average noise level might be around 40 to 50 dBA. Time of day can make a big difference in terms of the overall noise level. There is the Day-Night average level (Ldn) and the Community Noise Equivalent Level (CNEL), used to help compare cities since these metrics encompass the variations between daytime and nighttime noise levels.

A noisy urban or city area could be 60 to possibly 80 dBA, likely being at the higher point during daytime. When you are standing on the street and listening to the city noises, they can somewhat get bundled together and you might not be able to readily distinguish any particular sound. There tends to be a somewhat steady level of ambient noises that come at you. Some of the noises are nearby, while other sounds are coming from quite a distance.

While wandering around NYC, I felt as though the skyscrapers were able to at times magnify sounds that were quite a distance away from me. Construction sounds from several blocks away were able to travel in and around the giant buildings. It was as though I might be in a canyon and have echoing sounds that made their way from miles away.

The noises seemed to be continuous. There was little if any breaks in the drumbeat of sounds. Even at night time, while in my hotel room, the street noises continued all night long. Yes, I had the windows tightly closed, including drawing rather heavy curtains. Still, in spite of those aspects at blocking out the street sounds, it was immediately apparent that I was trying to sleep in a city that doesn't.

There are also sounds that momentarily appear and can be attention getting. For example, the sound of a siren coming from a police car, an ambulance, or a fire truck. If you aren't used to routinely and frequently hearing those sounds, it catches you ear right away, and you look to see what is coming on. Given the large populace in NYC, the odds of hearing a siren nearly all of the time is pretty high. During my stay, there were few stretches of time for which I could not hear the wail of a siren, either one that was close to me or one that might have been several blocks away.

I remember a major construction project that was going to take place in Los Angeles and there was some vocal concern about how noises from the construction might impact a nearby school and children's playground. At the time, I was working in that area and could see from my upper-floor office the dirt lot that the new retail space was proposed to be built upon. Just across the street there were elementary school children that would come outside for recess.

I pondered the massive amount of heavy equipment that would be rolled into the dirt lot and how much noise it would make. There was some demolition needed to remove the remnants of prior structures. The site itself would need to be graded and some excavation done. Once the actual building began getting constructed, there would be the mix of power tools, hand tools, generators, and a slew of other sounds coming from that site. Until I had seen a formal report undertaken about the dangers of those noises, I hadn't thought about what it might do to those children and adults at the nearby school and playground.

Noises can of course harm our ears, limiting our ability to hear. In addition, noises can be distracting and dilute or undermine attention. I had wondered whether the school children would be able to concentrate on their class work if they were continually being bombarded by outdoor noises. They probably would also have a hard time hearing the teacher. Imagine trying to take notes of a lecture on math or history, and you can only hear about one of every three words being uttered by the instructor.

According to the Environmental Protection Agency (EPA), noise pollution is a serious issue in the United States. There is a somewhat defacto nationwide noise pollution policy as enacted by the Noise Control Act of 1972. There are numerous local and state ordinances and policies about noise pollution. For federal highways, the Federal Highway Administration (FHWA) promulgates highway noise pollution rules as per the Congressional Federal-Aid Highway Act of 1970.

I've already mentioned that noise pollution could harm your hearing and can possibly impair the cognitive aspects of learning by children, which seem sufficiently important qualms to consider, yet there are other equally serious consequences too. Some studies suggest a link between noise pollution and the potential for having heart disease, or for having other ailments like high blood pressure, can be bad for your overall health. There are likely a plethora of adverse health consequences that we can list due to noise pollution.

I'll add that disrupted sleep is one of those, which made me somewhat dulled in my efforts during my stay there in NYC and I felt groggy at times. I don't want to make light of the matter, and I suppose it could also be that I was out partying with conference attendees until the late hours. In any case, allow me to emphasize, noise pollution is serious stuff.

When I bring up the topic of noise pollution, the usual reaction is a kind of surprise and say-what response. People are used to discussing air pollution, which they would readily agree is bad. People are aware of the dangers of water pollution and would readily agree it is bad. Noise pollution is a topic they often are unsure about. Noises? You are worried about noises, they ask? How bad can it be?

For most people, probably there is little or no concern about noise pollution in their everyday lives. They often realize that at a rock concert they are possibly harming their ears and therefore voluntarily engaging in a noise pollution moment. Same might be the case when going to a football game or basketball game at a stadium jam packed with screaming fans. Otherwise, they might hear the occasional jackhammer or siren, and not put much thought or concern toward noise pollution.

Those New Yorkers that I walked around with to get some pizza and enjoy the sights of the town, well, they by-and-large shrugged their shoulders about the noises and the noise pollution. They would wave their hands and arms in the air and say to me, "what you gonna do?" in exasperation. To them, the noises are as expected. The noises mean that their place is vibrant and alive.

They've already seen many efforts to curtail traffic, usually due to air pollution concerns. They've seen efforts to stop construction projects, often due to over-population concerns and the city crowding that can occur. Having dealt with numerous causes and concerns, they are as much "tone deaf" to those matters as they are to the noises of the city itself. They concede there is noise pollution, yet don't believe it is serious enough to do anything drastic and also tend to be unaware of what could be done about it anyway, other than merely bringing the place to a screeching (noisy) halt.

One aspect that many locals might not know is that there are ways to fight back against noise pollution. Typically, it involves contacting your local city noise enforcement team, consisting of government workers that can officially check on a noise polluter and do something about it, including fining the noise offender or taking other legal actions against them. You would not normally use an emergency number such as 911 to report such noise pollution instances, and instead would likely use some government reporting number such as 311.

In the case of NYC, they receive an average of around 800 reported noise complaints per day. This is likely just the tip of the iceberg in terms of how many people are genuinely frustrated and concerned about noise pollution aspects. Most people aren't aware that you can report the matter. Plus, those that are aware might not believe it is worth the effort to complain.

A primary reason that reporting a noise pollution instance might seem not worthwhile can be due to the transitory nature of a noise pollution occurrence.

Perhaps you have someone nearby your home that is making an incredible racket, and it is driving you nuts, along with the potential harm to your ears and those of passerby's. Suppose though that it is road repair crew and they are going to be done in a day or two.

By the time that an official noise pollution inspector comes out to your neighborhood to look into the complaint, the road repair crew might be long gone. There's not much that the inspector can do at that juncture. Generally, unless they can catch the noise polluter in the act, it is going to be difficult to formally try to fine them or take other action against them. You might carp that the noise level was outrageous, but without something more official and definitive, it's not likely to cut the mustard.

I'm guessing that at some point in your lifetime you've had a noisy crowd at a party in the house next door to you or that's across the street. Those socially generated noises are often handled by the police, prompted to respond by a neighbor calling 911 to complain about the ruckus. Normally, the police will ask the offenders to quiet down, likely generating compliance, and the momentary act of noise pollution is then abated. Persistent noise complaints about a particular house that has become the block's party destination are more likely to be able get a noise pollution case against them.

Earlier in my career, I bought a small house (it was all I could afford at the time!) in a packed neighborhood that was just a few blocks from a local main street that had lots of restaurants and bars. One aspect that I had not known and nor calculated was that on Friday nights and Saturday nights many residents would wander down to the main street, drink liquor feverishly, and then drunkenly come back to their domiciles.

Home owners such as myself were trying to keep the neighborhood in good shape and desired to maintain our property values as a real estate investment. The renters though did not necessarily care about property values. They would get home after hitting the bars, and proceed to party like crazy, all night long. Loud music. Loud voices. Screaming, yelling. Having a good old time, until they seemed to fall asleep in their drunken stupor by maybe 4 a.m. or so.

In one sense, this was not a transitory matter like the example earlier of a road repair crew that shows up for a day or two and then is gone. You could set your watch by the regularity of the noise pollution arising each late Friday and Saturday evening. I contacted the city to find out what could be done and there didn't seem to be much that I could do. They offered to come out and detect the noise, which was feasible because of its predictability, and that they could contact the owner of the property to officially notify (and hopefully scare) the owners into getting their renters to be more thoughtful.

It was not especially effective. Eventually, I opted to move, for mainly other reasons such as wanting a bigger house and tried to sell my small house. Darned if many of the potential buyers already knew about the noise issues on Friday and Saturday nights. They tried to talk me down on my asking price because of it. Plus, in California, there are requirements about reporting known hazards or other issues about a property you are selling, and so it came out in that manner too.

One of the houses that I was looking to buy was in a fortunately quiet suburban neighborhood, which I confirmed by talking with my potential neighbors, asking them if there were any noisy heathens in the area. Notably, I had wised up to the noise factor as a criterion for buying a house.

I purposely went to see the house on a variety of days and times, wanting to gauge whether there was anything unusual that maybe occurs depending upon the day of the week or the time of day. Turns out that the backyard of the house was butted up to a fence, and on the other side of the fence was a street that most of the time was lightly used.

During one of my random visits, I surprisingly discovered a whole bunch of traffic that was flowing down that street. Not far from this neighborhood was a trucking company that kept a slew of large-sized trucks in their parking lot. Unbeknownst to me, those trucks would routinely use that otherwise quiet street to leave the trucking yard and do the same when coming back to the trucking yard. The noise of these lumbering trucks coming along that normally quiet street was deafening.

In addition, you've likely felt vibrations from loud sounds, well, those trucks caused a tremendous vibration, partially due to the sounds of the trucks and also due to the heavy weight as they rumbled down the street behind my house. Of course, I realize that every home is likely to have something undesirable about it, but this was one of several marks against this particular property, so I opted not to buy it. I had no interest in trading the weekend party noises for instead the weekday morning and late afternoon barreling trucks noises.

Notice that throughout this discussion of noise pollution, one aspect that keeps coming up involves the detection of the noise pollution.

First and foremost, you have to realize that the noise pollution is happening. Furthermore, it is crucial to narrow down what the cause of the noise pollution is. Just having a hunch is not sufficient. For any kind of formal redress of abating the noise pollution, you'll need a rock-sold form of proof that the noises are occurring, the degree of the noises, the frequency and duration, and then if you want to go after someone, you'll need to figure out what or who is causing the noise.

As indicated earlier, it can be problematic to do this because of:

- You might not be fully aware that noise pollution is occurring and might have become used to it or consider it nonthreatening.

- You might not have any reliable means of formally detecting the noises and nor are registering them to know how bad they are.

- The noises might be blended with an array of noises and you are unable to readily isolate the worst of the noises from the others in the mix.

- You might not be able to trace the various noises to definitive corresponding sources.

- And so on.

There's an interesting study being undertaken at NYU and Ohio State University that seeks to sound out the noise pollution issue in New York City, funded partially by an NSF grant (researchers include Bello, Silva, Nov, Dubois, Arora, Salamon, Mydlarz, and Doraiswamy). They have been putting together a system they shrewdly call SONYC (Sounds Of New York City). Via the development of specialized listening devices, they have so far deployed 56 of the sensors in various locations of NYC, including Greenwich Village, Manhattan, Brooklyn, Queens, and other areas. I'll have to keep my eyes peeled to spot one, the next time I make a trip to NYC.

Their acoustic sensor is relatively inexpensive, costing to-date about $80 each and with the hope of further reducing the cost, which is crucial if there is a desire to deploy such devices on a widespread basis. Affordability of being able to conduct a noise pollution watchdog capability is a key factor in being able to undertake such initiatives.

They are using the somewhat ubiquitous Raspberry Pi processor and outfitted it with a custom-built MEMS (Microelectromechanical Microphone). The MEMS can detect an acoustic range of 32 dBA to 120 dBA. To try and ensure that this low-end low-priced component is believable, they are calibrating it against more expensive precision-grade sound-level meters.

These SONYC project devices are small and able to be placed on ledges, attached to poles, affixed to buildings, and placed in other areas that might be handy for detecting noise pollution. Besides doing 24x7 continuous monitoring, they have also setup the devices to capture 10-seconds worth of audio at random intervals.

The snippets of audio are especially useful for another key aspect to their efforts, namely the use of Machine Learning (ML) to analyze noises and the collected sounds data.

Many of you are likely familiar with the use of Machine Learning or Deep Learning (DL) for use on images, such as the famous examples of being able to spot an image of a dog or a cat inside a captured visual picture. Typically using large-scale convolutional neural networks, there are numerous applied systems and research efforts involved in further enhancing the ability for automation to detect visual elements in images and video. Facial recognition is perhaps one of the most well-known examples.

I'd bet that fewer of you are aware of the use of Machine Learning or Deep Learning on the use of audio data. It's certainly an interesting and difficult problem to try and ferret out details within an audio stream or snippet.

The problem can be made easier if you decide to try and decipher the audio of a guitar player and a flute player. If we have known sources of the audio and they each are distinctive, and if the recorded audio is clear cut and has little noise or overwhelming background sounds, and they are relatively stationary and persistent, this is a relatively easy Machine Learning of Deep Learning solvable circumstance.

On the other hand, consider the widely varying sounds recorded by a low-end audio device that is sitting on a ledge of a second story building adjacent to New York Times square. You are going to get quite a diverse mixture of sounds. The objects generating the sounds are likely to be in motion and not necessarily stationary. The sounds will come and go, at times being heard well and other times barely audible. There will be such a muddling of sounds that it will be arduous to tell them apart from each other.

Can you pick out of that mercurial swath of audio the kind of object or artifact producing each of the noises, doing so with a high probability and also differentiate it from the other sounds? Nontrivial.

Assume too that you aren't told beforehand what those objects or artifacts are.

You can certainly guess beforehand that there might be construction sounds, traffic sounds, the sounds of people talking and yelling, and so on. This can be helpful as a means to beforehand try to train a Machine Learning or Deep Learning system to try and identify the noises.

For the SONYC study, the researchers opted to see if they could do some labeling of data, providing therefore a leg-up for their Machine Learning training efforts. As a type of experiment, they sought participants via Amazon's Mechanical Turk, amassing over 500 people that aided annotating of the audio data presented.

The researchers had also developed a visual aid and were exploring how it could perhaps further enable the annotating process by the human labelers. The audio data was subject to various transformations and the researchers have helpfully made their soundscape tool available as open source.

Their study touches on a number of fascinating elements. The training of the Machine Learning or Deep Learning capability brings up the notion of doing crowdsourced audio soundscape annotating. On the one hand, the crowdsourced approach might ultimately be sufficient in being able to train the ML or DL, and then no longer be needed.

Or, one could possibly argue that you don't need the ML or DL and should just use humans for analyzing such audio data, but this is somewhat backward thinking, I'd say, and the use of automation seems a more inspired and likely effective, efficient, and scalable method.

In the case of this particular study, I am guessing that some of you might be wondering whether it might be possible to use modern-day smartphones as a means of capturing the sounds that might then be analyzed by the ML or DL for noise pollution purposes. The use of a smartphone as a sound collecting device presents other problems, including the lack of precision and calibration for sound sensing, along with whether the smartphones would be used by humans as they are walking around or opting to try and point out a noisy place, offering therefore likely intermittent, inconsistent, and somewhat suspect audio data.

The proposed use of low-priced and yet palatable devices offers a consistency and reliability factor and could be placed in static locations for sustained periods of time. In contrast, some prior efforts on noise pollution detection have attempted to use relatively higher-end sound meters, which tend to be costlier and often not built to withstand the rigors of longer periods of outdoor postings.

It is useful to consider the rise of edge computing in this matter, namely that we are moving toward an era when their will be relatively smaller sized computing devices distributed around our roadways and infrastructure. This also coincides with the rise of the Internet of Things (IoT), another convergence toward dealing with situations wherein there is a need or value in having computing and sensory devices available all around us and not so confined or restricted.

What does this have to do with AI self-driving cars?

At the Cybernetic AI Self-Driving Car Institute, we are developing AI software for self-driving cars. One aspect that we've been actively exploring is the use of audio sensors on a self-driving car to aid in the AI being able to drive the vehicle, such as detecting sirens of police cars and other matters. The noise pollution studies dovetail into this kind of effort.

Allow me to elaborate.

I'd like to first clarify and introduce the notion that there are varying levels of AI self-driving cars. The topmost level is considered Level 5. A Level 5 self-driving car is one that is being driven by the AI and there is no human driver involved. For the design of Level 5 self-driving cars, the auto makers are even removing the gas pedal, brake pedal, and steering wheel, since those are contraptions used by human drivers. The Level 5 self-driving car is not being driven by a human and nor is there an expectation that a human driver will be present in the self-driving car. It's all on the shoulders of the AI to drive the car.

For self-driving cars less than a Level 5, there must be a human driver present in the car. The human driver is currently considered the responsible party for the acts of the car. The AI and the human driver are co-sharing the driving task. In spite of this co-sharing, the human is supposed to remain fully immersed into the driving task and be ready at all times to perform the driving task. I've repeatedly warned about the dangers of this co-sharing arrangement and predicted it will produce many untoward results.

Let's focus herein on the true Level 5 self-driving car. Much of the comments apply to the less than Level 5 self-driving cars too, but the fully autonomous AI self-driving car will receive the most attention in this discussion.

Here's the usual steps involved in the AI driving task:
- Sensor data collection and interpretation
- Sensor fusion
- Virtual world model updating
- AI action planning
- Car controls command issuance

Another key aspect of AI self-driving cars is that they will be driving on our roadways in the midst of human driven cars too. There are some pundits of AI self-driving cars that continually refer to a utopian world in which there are only AI self-driving cars on the public roads. Currently there are about 250+ million conventional cars in the United States alone, and those cars are not going to magically disappear or become true Level 5 AI self-driving cars overnight.

Indeed, the use of human driven cars will last for many years, likely many decades, and the advent of AI self-driving cars will occur while there are still human driven cars on the roads. This is a crucial point since this means that the AI of self-driving cars needs to be able to contend with not just other AI self-driving cars, but also contend with human driven cars. It is easy to envision a simplistic and rather unrealistic world in which all AI self-driving cars are politely interacting with each other and being civil about roadway interactions. That's not what is going to be happening for the foreseeable future. AI self-driving cars and human driven cars will need to be able to cope with each other.

Returning to the topic of audio soundscapes and how it pertains to AI self-driving cars, along with how it pertains to noise pollution research advances, I'll address these matters next.

First, let's consider that the interior of AI self-driving cars will have audio microphones, doing so to allow the human occupants to be able to converse with the AI system driving the self-driving car. Similar to the popular use of Siri and Alexa of today, there will be Natural Language Processing (NLP) verbalization components of the AI that will interact with passengers.

Some falsely assume that this interaction with the AI will be confined to just providing an indicated destination of where the passenger wants to be driven. I have repeatedly debunked this myth and pointed out that there is a slew of conversational aspects that will be needed by true AI self-driving cars.

Consider the dynamic nature of a conversation with a human chauffeur and it posits some of the interaction that will be desired, including discussions about intermediary destinations, changes in destination endpoints, smoothness of the drive, and other such facets.

I realize that some immediately jump on this notion and say that they've been in cabs and ridesharing vehicles wherein the human driver was unable or unwilling to carry on a conversation. As such, this seems to imply that it is sufficient to have AI that can only do simple kinds of verbal acts and take essentially rudimentary commands from a passenger.

Yes, we've all had those kinds of being-driven experiences, and it might be satisfactory for the initial and crude versions of AI self-driving cars, but this will wear thin quickly and human occupants will be seeking more elaborated dialogue. Those auto makers and tech firms that can provide such AI NLP will undoubtedly see greater interest by those wishing or willing to ride in an AI self-driving car.

Mark my words, the voice is the AI self-driving car, from the perspective of the human rider. Anyone that lets the voice aspects be handled by someone other than the auto maker or tech firm will be ultimately second-fiddle in the eyes of those riding in AI self-driving cars.

Most of the auto makers and tech firms are gradually realizing the importance of the interior audio interaction aspects of an AI self-driving car and we'll be seeing soon enough strident advances in that area.

In contrast, let's consider the use of exterior audio microphones and an AI self-driving car.

Few of the auto makers and tech firms are giving much attention to the use of externally focused audio microphones for an AI self-driving car. Indeed, they would generally classify the use of such sensory capabilities as an edge or corner problem. An edge or corner problem is one that is considered not at the core of what you are trying to solve. It is something that can be dealt with at a later time. You aim to get the core solved and then come back around to deal with the edges or corners.

Some also refer to these edge or corner cases as "the long tail" of an AI system.

Why is the use of external audio microphones tossed into the edge or corner cases basket? Mainly due to the aspect that the AI developers already have their hands full on the other elements of making an AI self-driving car work as hoped for. In that sense, yes, they are focused on what they consider core. Having an AI self-driving car that can navigate a road without hitting things, that's core. Having an AI self-driving car that abides by the rules-of-the-road, that's core.

Dealing with the sounds that are outside of the AI self-driving car are, well, interesting, but not essential, right now, in the view of many AI developers. I have predicted that ultimately when the other features of AI self-driving cars are all about the same, it will become more apparent that we've missed dealing with the vital and quite important use of sound as a sensory element for driving a car.

One obvious example of how external sounds are crucial involves the sirens of police cars, ambulances, fire trucks, and other emergency vehicles. Human drivers are supposed to be alert for the sound of such sirens. When such a siren is heard, the human driver knows to be cautious of any emergency vehicles that might be in their vicinity. The louder the siren sound, likely the closer the vehicle is to the car.

I'm sure that you've had moments whereby you were sitting at a red light and heard a siren, coming from some distance away, faint at first. As you waited for your green light, you heard the siren wailing and getting louder and louder. You readily deduced that the vehicle making the siren sound was getting closer to you. The light goes green and you hesitate to drive into the intersection, knowing that at any moment an emergency vehicle might come zipping through the intersection.

I realize that some of you might say that you often don't hear the siren, even though it might be wailing, and that you instead rely upon your eyes to see the flashing lights of the emergency vehicle. You might also use as a clue that other cars nearby are coming to a halt or pulling over, which is another indicator that perhaps an emergency vehicle is coming and maybe they heard it while you did not.

The point being that some AI developers try to argue that being able to hear a siren is nice, but not essential. As long as the vision system of the AI self-driving car is able to identify emergency vehicles, whether those vehicles are being heard or not is not key and merely icing on the cake. Likewise, they emphasize that the radar and the LIDAR are bound to detect a fast-moving vehicle and be able to add a warning to the AI action planning component that likely an emergency vehicle is nearby.

It is true of course that people often do not hear the sirens of emergency vehicles. I think you would also agree that this is a disadvantage in that waiting until you can see an emergency vehicle is cutting the ice pretty thin.

Whereas you might see the emergency vehicle only a few split seconds before it rushes into that intersection ahead of you, your ability to hear the siren would have given you a much greater early warning to be watchful of the speeding vehicle.

One would hope that with AI self-driving cars we are trying to make them as safe as feasible. Omitting the use of a sense that us human drivers use, the sense of hearing, seems like a rather apparent omission. I'm not going to try to further justify herein the external audio microphone as a sensory device for AI self-driving cars and will let stand my prediction that it will become a heralded component once the industry wakes-up to its vital function.

In some ways, I argue that the use of external audio capture and interpretation is somewhat like the use of shadows that can be captured by camera images. A focus on shadows is called computational periscopy and provides an added element to try and further improve the safety of the AI driving, providing the possibility of early detection of possibly dire situations. Whether you consider it to be simply icing on the cake, or whether it is an essential element, depends upon the eye of the beholder.

Another sensory aspect that is being neglected for AI self-driving cars involves the use of smelling or odor detection. I admit this is indeed an edge or corner case and not especially close to the core aspects of an AI system for a self-driving car. Nonetheless, the potential use of e-noses or olfactory sensors is yet another means for the AI to have a better chance at detecting the environment in which it is driving, and be a safer driving system than otherwise without such sensors.

So, let's agree for the moment that though the auto makers and tech firms are not jumping yet on the bandwagon of using exterior audio microphones, they will gradually and inextricably get there.

I have mentioned that these sensors could aid the detection of sirens, doing so as a heads-up about an approaching emergency vehicle. That's just one way in which the exterior audio microphones might be useful.

Another practical use would be the ability to undertake a verbal dialogue with humans outside of the self-driving car.

A human might be standing outside of the AI self-driving car and ask the self-driving car to move back a few feet, perhaps because the AI self-driving car has come up to drop-off someone at a hotel valet area and gotten overly close to another car waiting to be parked.

Or, perhaps a human is standing at a ridesharing waiting area and wants to potentially use the AI self-driving car as a ridesharing service. Rather than having to convey the request via a smartphone, which is the way we commonly do so today, the human might simply speak to the AI self-driving car. This would be akin to trying to speak to a cabbie that is standing next to their waiting cab.

In essence, we can come up with a sizable number of useful reasons to have exterior audio microphones as added sensors on an AI self-driving car.

The other aspect about such audio sensors is that it will not unduly increase the weight of the self-driving car, a factor always to be considered when adding additional sensors and will only marginally increase the cost. Most such audio sensors will be relatively small in size, relatively lightweight, relatively low in cost, and can be included into the car body or added-on without too much painstaking redesign of the self-driving car.

Some envision that if the auto makers and tech firms don't build such sensors into the self-driving cars, there might be a thriving add-on kit marketplace to augment an AI self-driving car with such audio sensors. I am somewhat skeptical about the viability of doing such add-ons. Nonetheless, I do concur that there will be a movement towards including audio sensors, one way or another.

When will the audio microphone sensors be active on an AI self-driving car? My answer is straightforward, all of the time. There are some advocates of audio sensors that say they should only be sparingly in use. Their concern is that if you have these audio sensors on all of the time, it implies that the AI self-driving car is potentially capturing all sounds wherever it drives. This might be a kind of privacy invasion.

Thought I am sympathetic to the privacy aspects, and they are certainly worthy of figuring out what to do, I am somewhat puzzled that these same concerns aren't voiced about the cameras that are continually capturing visual images and video. The same can be said about the radar sensors, the ultrasonic sensors, the LIDAR, and so on. In other words, I don't see why the audio is any special case. To me, it is part of the larger privacy picture of what are we going to do about AI self-driving cars that are capturing everything they detect during their driving journeys.

It's a momentous matter of privacy that no one is yet wrestling with on any macroscopic scale.

Some say that the cameras and other non-audio sensors are more essential to the driving of the self-driving car, therefore they argue that let's at least curtail something that otherwise is not so essential. This takes us back to my earlier argument about whether or not you believe that the exterior audio capture and interpretation is vital or not. I think it is vital.

In any case, I'm betting that the audio microphones will likely be working whenever the self-driving car is active, and potentially when it isn't active too. Why would the audio detection be functioning when the car is parked and the engine is presumably shut-off? The obvious answer is to wake-up the AI of the self-driving car. Just as Alexa and Siri are continually scanning for a wake-up word, so would the AI of the self-driving car.

In theory, this audio awakening might be "ignoring" any sounds it hears until it detects the wake-up word. This is something that many of today's speech recognition systems claim to do. In that manner, one might assume that the AI self-driving car is not recording every utterance that occurs near to it, and nor capturing any and all sounds around it, while it is in a sleeping state. But, that's something that we've yet to see what the auto makers and tech firms are going to do, and whether or not they plan to be recording such audio or merely scanning and dumping it right away.

One aspect to keep in mind is that AI self-driving cars are likely to be running nearly non-stop 24-x7, as much as possible. The logic being that if you have an AI self-driving car that does not need a human driver, you might as well put the self-driving car to use as much as you can. No need to worry about whether you have a driver available, since you always and permanently do have the AI there.

For purposes of being able to afford an AI self-driving car, it is anticipated that if the costs of an AI self-driving car are high, you would want to maximize the revenue potential of the self-driving car. If you own an AI self-driving car, you might use it to get to work, and then while at the office, you would have your AI self-driving car roaming the streets as a ridesharing service. When you needed it to go get lunch or drive you home, you take it out of the ridesharing pool and use it as your own car.

The reason I point out the non-stop use, along with the roaming aspects for ridesharing purposes, brings us once again to the aspect of what the audio sensors are going to be hearing while on an AI self-driving car. Presumably, those audio sensors are going to capture sounds throughout the day and night, doing so wherever the AI self-driving car happens to roam.

We are now ready to discuss noise pollution abatement and the advent of AI self-driving cars.

My discussion about the SONYC approach indicated that there is noise pollution that exists and has health and economic adverse consequences, and to try and aid the abatement of noise pollution we need a means to be able to quantify the nature of the noises and be able to detect them, along with pinning down the sources of the noises.

One such approach involves the effort by the SONYC researchers of developing and deploying low-priced sensory devices that could be placed throughout a geographical area to get a systematic collection of the noises and then be further leveraged via the application of appropriate Machine Learning or Deep Learning systems to analyze and interpret the audio data.

Another potential approach involves using the exterior audio data being captured by AI self-driving cars.

Imagine an area like downtown Los Angeles. Suppose we had a slew of AI self-driving cars that were roaming up and down the streets, serving as ridesharing services. While driving around, they are capturing visual imagery data, radar data, LIDAR data, ultrasonic data, and let's say also audio data.

Each of those AI self-driving cars has a potential treasure trove of collected audio data. Of course, the audio data might be either top-quality or low-quality, depending upon the type of audio sensors included into the AI self-driving car. How many such audio sensors on any given AI self-driving car will also be a factor, along with where on the self-driving car those audio sensors are placed.

I am not suggesting that it is axiomatic that the exterior audio sensors will be able to provide valuable audio data for noise pollution abatement purposes. But it is one additional avenue worthy of consideration.

The on-board AI system of the AI self-driving car might have an added software component to aid in analyzing the audio data that is being collected, doing so in real-time.

I realize that we need to ascertain whether this effort is worthwhile or not, in the sense that if you are using the precious and resource-limited computer processors to do this kind of work, while the self-driving car is in-motion, it seems unlikely to be worthwhile doing so if it somehow starves the core driving functions of the AI system that is trying to drive the car in real-time.

Another approach would be for the audio data to be pushed up to the cloud of the auto maker or tech firm.

This is generally going to be happening for the other sensory collected data. Via the use of Over-The-Air (OTA) electronic communications, the auto makers and tech firms will be collecting volumes of driving related data. The OTA will also be used to push down to the AI self-driving car various patches and updates.

Since AI self-driving cars will likely be separated into "fleets," meaning that a particular auto maker might have their own cloud, while other auto makers have their own respective clouds, it might make trying to cohesively bring together all of the collected audio data somewhat problematic. This would need to be worked out with the auto makers and tech firms.

There are a number of interesting twists and turns to this notion.

One important element is that the AI self-driving cars are going to be in-motion most of the time. Whereas the use of low-priced geographically placed audio sensors will typically be fixed in place for some lengthy period of time, the audio sensor on the AI self-driving cars are going to be on the journey of wherever the AI self-driving car goes.

Can this audio data be useful when it is being captured while in-motion on an AI self-driving car? I am not asking about whether it can be useful for real-time analyses, which I've already mentioned, but instead pondering whether the audio data collected might be skewed in ways that are as a result of the audio being captured by an in-motion audio sensor.

It is a potentially interesting Machine Learning or Deep Learning problem to include that the audio data was captured while the device itself was in-motion. This would seem to also likely require added forms of audio data transformations.

We also need to consider the triangulation aspects.

I am referring to the notion that on any given AI self-driving car there might be several of the exterior audio sensors. It would seem sensible to try and compare the audio captured by those multiple sensors and try to piece together what the self-driving car has captured of the noises that surround it. The audio sensor data captured at the front of the self-driving car could be meshed or triangulated with the audio sensors data captured at the rear of the self-driving car, and so on.

There would also be an interesting problem of triangulating the audio sensor data from a multitude of AI self-driving cars. Suppose that there are four AI self-driving cars that each drive past a construction site in downtown Los Angeles, doing so at the same moment in time. Two are headed north, two are going southbound, and all four on the same street. Let's triangulate those audio data captures to see what they might indicate about the noises coming from the construction site.

Making the matter more complex, let's say that nearly a hundred AI self-driving cars drove past that construction site in a 24-hour period, encompassing daytime and nighttime sound recordings. Some of the self-driving cars were on the street in front of the construction site, some went on the street behind it, and some were on streets blocks away from the construction site.

That's quite a triangulation problem. You have variability in where the self-driving cars captured the audio aspects, you have variability in their motion aspects (sometimes perhaps stuck in traffic and nearby to the site for minutes, while other times zipping past at higher speeds), you have variability in the time of day, you have variability in how many self-driving cars were able to capture such audio data, and so on.

In a manner of speaking, you could say that the noise data collection is nearly "free" because the AI self-driving cars are going to presumably have the audio sensors anyway, if you agree with me that they should. Though the audio sensors weren't necessarily included in the AI self-driving cars to aid noise pollution abatement, it is an added benefit to having those audio sensors for their otherwise purposes for the AI self-driving car functions.

Could the audio sensors of the AI self-driving cars be used entirely in lieu of using stationary fixed-in-place audio sensors? Maybe, maybe not.

The odds are that with the rather gradual adoption of AI self-driving cars, you would for quite some time in the future have a rather spotty collection of the noises in any given area. In other words, with so few AI self-driving cars, and their random chance of being in any particular place, you would have large gaps of audio and those gaps might undermine the noise abatement usage.

If you combined the AI self-driving cars collected audio data with the fixed-in-place audio sensors, it could be a helpful augmentation to those fixed-in-place audio sensors. Furthermore, it would be building perhaps towards a day when the saturation of AI self-driving cars in a given geographical areas is so high that you would be able to rely solely on the AI self-driving cars data and might not need the fixed-in-place sensors in that particular locale.

Conclusion

There is a potential that AI self-driving cars could aid the emerging noise pollution abatement efforts.

It admittedly is an uphill battle. AI self-driving cars have to be outfitted with audio sensors, which I've argued they should be anyway for the safety and other purposes of the AI driving a self-driving car. We can than tag along the already useful function of the audio sensors and add the potential for being servants in the war on noise pollution.

It's not clear whether the audio analyses for noise pollution would be viable in real-time if the AI self-driving car cannot spare the processing capabilities to do so. This might mean that the audio data for noise pollution abatement purposes is shared up to the cloud. Complications exist that the different auto makers will each have their own clouds and somehow an arrangement would need to be made to bring together that audio data.

There are lots of privacy issues to be dealt with in this audio data collection. Will the humans that own or use these AI self-driving cars be comfortable with having the exterior audio kept and used for these noise pollution abatement purposes. How much of the time and when will the audio data be captured from the sensors?

There is a slew of difficult technical issues to be dealt with too. How useful will audio data that is captured while an AI self-driving car is in-motion be? How hard will it be to triangulate the audio data of a single AI self-driving car, and then how hard would it be to do so for a myriad of self-driving cars, perhaps hundreds or thousands of such audio sensor equipped self-driving cars.

The amount of data would be possibly staggering. Even with compression trickery, you are still referring to the audio sensors collecting data potentially non-stop, every second and every minute and every hour of every day and doing so for hundreds or thousands of AI self-driving cars (ultimately, perhaps millions upon millions of self-driving cars). There might need to be newly devised "smart" ways of deciding what data to keep as it is essential for analysis purposes, versus what data can be discarded rather than carried around or shoveled up to the cloud.

Noise pollution for most people is relatively low on their list of pollution concerns. Unless the public perceives the value of undertaking noise abatement actions, there is likely little impetus for the auto makers and tech firms to consider how the audio sensors and audio data might be used for noise abatement purposes.

I suppose too that one might be somewhat worried that their own AI self-driving car is perhaps contributing to the noise problems, though this would seem not quite so worrisome as to fully scuttle the idea of using the audio sensor data to try and avert overall noise pollution.

In any case, the efforts to achieve noise pollution abatement are an avenue of improving the use of Machine Learning and Deep Learning for doing audio data pattern matching and analyses. For those purposes alone, it's a handy and helpful endeavor, let alone the noise abatement matter.

Those methods can be likely reused or borrowed for doing the types of audio data analyses that the auto makers and tech firms directly care about, such as separating out the sound of a siren from other city noises and trying to determine where the source is. That's the kind of noise analysis that makes abundant sense for the safety of an AI self-driving car and we need more efforts to enhance what are rather rudimentary capabilities today. I say, let's make some loud noise in favor of that.

APPENDIX

APPENDIX A
TEACHING WITH THIS MATERIAL

The material in this book can be readily used either as a supplemental to other content for a class, or it can also be used as a core set of textbook material for a specialized class. Classes where this material is most likely used include any classes at the college or university level that want to augment the class by offering thought provoking and educational essays about AI and self-driving cars.

In particular, here are some aspects for class use:

o   <u>Computer Science</u>. Studying AI, autonomous vehicles, etc.

o   <u>Business</u>. Exploring technology and it adoption for business.

o   <u>Sociology</u>. Sociological views on the adoption and advancement of technology.

Specialized classes at the undergraduate and graduate level can also make use of this material.

For each chapter, consider whether you think the chapter provides material relevant to your course topic. There is plenty of opportunity to get the students thinking about the topic and force them to decide whether they agree or disagree with the points offered and positions taken. I would also encourage you to have the students do additional research beyond the chapter material presented (I provide next some suggested assignments they can do).

RESEARCH ASSIGNMENTS ON THESE TOPICS

Your students can find background material on these topics, doing so in various business and technical publications. I list below the top ranked AI related journals. For business publications, I would suggest the usual culprits such as the Harvard Business Review, Forbes, Fortune, WSJ, and the like.

Here are some suggestions of homework or projects that you could assign to students:

a) Assignment for foundational AI research topic: Research and prepare a paper and a presentation on a specific aspect of Deep AI, Machine Learning, ANN, etc. The paper should cite at least 3 reputable sources. Compare and contrast to what has been stated in this book.

b) Assignment for the Self-Driving Car topic: Research and prepare a paper and Self-Driving Cars. Cite at least 3 reputable sources and analyze the characterizations. Compare and contrast to what has been stated in this book.

c) Assignment for a Business topic: Research and prepare a paper and a presentation on businesses and advanced technology. What is hot, and what is not? Cite at least 3 reputable sources. Compare and contrast to the depictions in this book.

d) Assignment to do a Startup: Have the students prepare a paper about how they might startup a business in this realm. They must submit a sound Business Plan for the startup. They could also be asked to present their Business Plan and so should also have a presentation deck to coincide with it.

You can certainly adjust the aforementioned assignments to fit to your particular needs and the class structure. You'll notice that I ask for 3 reputable cited sources for the paper writing based assignments. I usually steer students toward "reputable" publications, since otherwise they will cite some oddball source that has no credentials other than that they happened to write something and post it onto the Internet. You can define "reputable" in whatever way you prefer, for example some faculty think Wikipedia is not reputable while others believe it is reputable and allow students to cite it.

The reason that I usually ask for at least 3 citations is that if the student only does one or two citations they usually settle on whatever they happened to find the fastest. By requiring three citations, it usually seems to force them to look around, explore, and end-up probably finding five or more, and then whittling it down to 3 that they will actually use.

I have not specified the length of their papers, and leave that to you to tell the students what you prefer. For each of those assignments, you could end-up with a short one to two pager, or you could do a dissertation length paper. Base the length on whatever best fits for your class, and the credit amount of the assignment within the context of the other grading metrics you'll be using for the class.

I mention in the assignments that they are to do a paper and prepare a presentation. I usually try to get students to present their work. This is a good practice for what they will do in the business world. Most of the time, they will be required to prepare an analysis and present it. If you don't have the class time or inclination to have the students present, then you can of course cut out the aspect of them putting together a presentation.

If you want to point students toward highly ranked journals in AI, here's a list of the top journals as reported by *various citation counts sources* (this list changes year to year):

- o Communications of the ACM
- o Artificial Intelligence
- o Cognitive Science
- o IEEE Transactions on Pattern Analysis and Machine Intelligence
- o Foundations and Trends in Machine Learning
- o Journal of Memory and Language
- o Cognitive Psychology
- o Neural Networks
- o IEEE Transactions on Neural Networks and Learning Systems
- o IEEE Intelligent Systems
- o Knowledge-based Systems

GUIDE TO USING THE CHAPTERS

For each of the chapters, I provide next some various ways to use the chapter material. You can assign the tasks as individual homework assignments, or the tasks can be used with team projects for the class. You can easily layout a series of assignments, such as indicating that the students are to do item "a" below for say Chapter 1, then "b" for the next chapter of the book, and so on.

a) What is the main point of the chapter and describe in your own words the significance of the topic,

b) Identify at least two aspects in the chapter that you agree with, and support your concurrence by providing at least one other outside researched item as support; make sure to explain your basis for disagreeing with the aspects,

c) Identify at least two aspects in the chapter that you disagree with, and support your disagreement by providing at least one other outside researched item as support; make sure to explain your basis for disagreeing with the aspects,

d) Find an aspect that was not covered in the chapter, doing so by conducting outside research, and then explain how that aspect ties into the chapter and what significance it brings to the topic,

e) Interview a specialist in industry about the topic of the chapter, collect from them their thoughts and opinions, and readdress the chapter by citing your source and how they compared and contrasted to the material,

f) Interview a relevant academic professor or researcher in a college or university about the topic of the chapter, collect from them their thoughts and opinions, and readdress the chapter by citing your source and how they compared and contrasted to the material,

g) Try to update a chapter by finding out the latest on the topic, and ascertain whether the issue or topic has now been solved or whether it is still being addressed, explain what you come up with.

The above are all ways in which you can get the students of your class involved in considering the material of a given chapter. You could mix things up by having one of those above assignments per each week, covering the chapters over the course of the semester or quarter.

As a reminder, here are the chapters of the book and you can select whichever chapters you find most valued for your particular class:

Chapter Title

Companion Book By This Author

Advances in AI and Autonomous Vehicles:
Cybernetic Self-Driving Cars

Practical Advances in Artificial Intelligence (AI)
and Machine Learning
by
Dr. Lance B. Eliot, MBA, PhD

This title is available via Amazon and other book sellers

Companion Book By This Author

Self-Driving Cars:
"The Mother of All AI Projects"

by Dr. Lance B. Eliot, MBA, PhD

This title is available via Amazon and other book sellers

This title is available via Amazon and other book sellers

Companion Book By This Author

New Advances in AI Autonomous Driverless Cars Self-Driving Cars

by Dr. Lance B. Eliot, MBA, PhD

Chapter Title

This title is available via Amazon and other book sellers

Companion Book By This Author

Introduction to Driverless Self-Driving Cars

by Dr. Lance B. Eliot, MBA, PhD

This title is available via Amazon and other book sellers

<u>Companion Book By This Author</u>

Autonomous Vehicle Driverless Self-Driving Cars and Artificial Intelligence

by Dr. Lance B. Eliot, MBA, PhD

This title is available via Amazon and other book sellers

Companion Book By This Author

Transformative Artificial Intelligence Driverless Self-Driving Cars

by Dr. Lance B. Eliot, MBA, PhD

This title is available via Amazon and other book sellers

<u>Companion Book By This Author</u>

Disruptive Artificial Intelligence and Driverless Self-Driving Cars

by Dr. Lance B. Eliot, MBA, PhD

<u>Chapter Title</u>

This title is available via Amazon and other book sellers

Companion Book By This Author

State-of-the-Art
AI Driverless Self-Driving Cars

by Dr. Lance B. Eliot, MBA, PhD

Chapter Title

This title is available via Amazon and other book sellers

Companion Book By This Author

Top Trends in
AI Self-Driving Cars

by Dr. Lance B. Eliot, MBA, PhD

Chapter Title

This title is available via Amazon and other book sellers

Companion Book By This Author

AI Innovations and Self-Driving Cars

by Dr. Lance B. Eliot, MBA, PhD

<u>Chapter Title</u>

This title is available via Amazon and other book sellers

Companion Book By This Author

Crucial Advances for
AI Self-Driving Cars

by Dr. Lance B. Eliot, MBA, PhD

Chapter Title

This title is available via Amazon and other book sellers

This title is available via Amazon and other book sellers

Companion Book By This Author

Pioneering Advances for AI Driverless Cars

by Dr. Lance B. Eliot, MBA, PhD

This title is available via Amazon and other book sellers

Companion Book By This Author

Leading Edge Trends for AI Driverless Cars

by Dr. Lance B. Eliot, MBA, PhD

Chapter Title

This title is available via Amazon and other book sellers

Companion Book By This Author

The Cutting Edge of
AI Autonomous Cars

by Dr. Lance B. Eliot, MBA, PhD

This title is available via Amazon and other book sellers

Companion Book By This Author

The Next Wave of
AI Self-Driving Cars

by Dr. Lance B. Eliot, MBA, PhD

This title is available via Amazon and other book sellers

Companion Book By This Author

Revolutionary Innovations of AI Self-Driving Cars

by Dr. Lance B. Eliot, MBA, PhD

Chapter Title

This title is available via Amazon and other book sellers

This title is available via Amazon and other book sellers

Companion Book By This Author

Trailblazing Trends for **AI Self-Driving Cars**

by Dr. Lance B. Eliot, MBA, PhD

This title is available via Amazon and other book sellers

Companion Book By This Author

Ingenious Strides for
AI Driverless Cars

by Dr. Lance B. Eliot, MBA, PhD

This title is available via Amazon and other book sellers

Companion Book By This Author

AI Self-Driving Cars Inventiveness

by Dr. Lance B. Eliot, MBA, PhD

Chapter Title

This title is available via Amazon and other book sellers

<u>Companion Book By This Author</u>

Visionary Secrets of
AI Driverless Cars

by Dr. Lance B. Eliot, MBA, PhD

<u>Chapter Title</u>

This title is available via Amazon and other book sellers

<u>Companion Book By This Author</u>

Spearheading
AI Self-Driving Cars

by Dr. Lance B. Eliot, MBA, PhD

<u>Chapter Title</u>

This title is available via Amazon and other book sellers

253

Companion Book By This Author

Spurring
AI Self-Driving Cars

by Dr. Lance B. Eliot, MBA, PhD

Chapter Title

This title is available via Amazon and other book sellers

ABOUT THE AUTHOR

Dr. Lance B. Eliot, MBA, PhD is the CEO of Techbruim, Inc. and Executive Director of the Cybernetic AI Self-Driving Car Institute, and has over twenty years of industry experience including serving as a corporate officer in a billion dollar firm and was a partner in a major executive services firm. He is also a serial entrepreneur having founded, ran, and sold several high-tech related businesses. He previously hosted the popular radio show *Technotrends* that was also available on American Airlines flights via their in-flight audio program. Author or co-author of a dozen books and over 400 articles, he has made appearances on CNN, and has been a frequent speaker at industry conferences.

A former professor at the University of Southern California (USC), he founded and led an innovative research lab on Artificial Intelligence in Business. Known as the "AI Insider" his writings on AI advances and trends has been widely read and cited. He also previously served on the faculty of the University of California Los Angeles (UCLA), and was a visiting professor at other major universities. He was elected to the International Board of the Society for Information Management (SIM), a prestigious association of over 3,000 high-tech executives worldwide.

He has performed extensive community service, including serving as Senior Science Adviser to the Vice Chair of the Congressional Committee on Science & Technology. He has served on the Board of the OC Science & Engineering Fair (OCSEF), where he is also has been a Grand Sweepstakes judge, and likewise served as a judge for the Intel International SEF (ISEF). He served as the Vice Chair of the Association for Computing Machinery (ACM) Chapter, a prestigious association of computer scientists. Dr. Eliot has been a shark tank judge for the USC Mark Stevens Center for Innovation on start-up pitch competitions, and served as a mentor for several incubators and accelerators in Silicon Valley and Silicon Beach. He served on several Boards and Committees at USC, including having served on the Marshall Alumni Association (MAA) Board in Southern California.

Dr. Eliot holds a PhD from USC, MBA, and Bachelor's in Computer Science, and earned the CDP, CCP, CSP, CDE, and CISA certifications. Born and raised in Southern California, and having traveled and lived internationally, he enjoys scuba diving, surfing, and sailing.

ADDENDUM

Spurring
AI Self-Driving Cars

*Practical Advances in Artificial Intelligence (AI)
and Machine Learning*

By
Dr. Lance B. Eliot, MBA, PhD

—————

For supplemental materials of this book, visit:
www.ai-selfdriving-cars.guru

For special orders of this book, contact:
LBE Press Publishing
Email: LBE.Press.Publishing@gmail.com

www.ingramcontent.com/pod-product-compliance
Lightning Source LLC
Chambersburg PA
CBHW051047050326
40690CB00006B/627